Companion on Life's Journey

A Book of Prayers and Readings

Companion on Life's Journey

A Book of Prayers and Readings

Compiled and edited by Bede Hubbard

COLLINS

Collins Liturgical Publications
8 Grafton Street, London W1X 3LA

Collins Liturgical in the USA
Icehouse One — 401, 151 Union Street
San Francisco, CA 94111-1299

Distributed in Ireland by
Educational Company of Ireland
21 Talbot Street, Dublin 1

Collins Liturgical Australia
PO Box 316, Blackburn, Victoria 3130

Collins Liturgical New Zealand
PO Box 1, Auckland

ISBN 0 00 599102 1

First published 1987. This edition published 1987 by Collins Liturgical Publications.

Illustrations: Stations of the Cross by Pierre-Paul Rioux, photographed by Clément Claveau.

Design and layout: Gilles Lépine, Denis De Carufel and Alred Dupuy.

Acknowledgements are found at the end of the book.

Printed in Great Britain by William Collins PLC, Glasgow

Contents

Introduction

The angel Raphael said to the elderly Tobias, "Do not be afraid. I will be a companion on the journey. All will be well. The way is safe."

Tobit 5:20

The prayers and reflections in *Companion on Life's Journey* were collected not only for older Catholics but for everyone who is aware of how life is indeed a brief journey. This awareness may have come through children leaving home, death of a friend, leaving a job, moving to a new home, personal illness — it could be the result of any of the many occasions in life when we have to say good-by to the familiar and greet the unknown.

Awareness that life is passing and we are simple travellers helps to make our yesterdays comforting, strengthening reminders of past courage, loyalty and love. We need our memories of yesterday: where have we come from? how did we get here? what were the best roads? But travellers also need a vision of tomorrow. Otherwise we will never move on, never dream about the journey's end, never summon the hope and strength we need for letting today pass and become one more step in life's voyage.

By being reminded that life is a journey we become more aware of how we are called to follow the ancient example of God's Chosen People. Like them, forsaking the land of idols, we are called to pass over into a new land of promise where God is not an immobile monument but the Spirit living within human hearts. Our exodus, the same as that of the Chosen People, means we too must be ready to move on, prepared to leave possessions behind. We trust the One who, when we are comfortably settled is the Unknown, but when we are lost in the wilderness is revealed as the One Who Is With Us.

Seeing life as a journey is another way of saying we are on pilgrimage, travelling together for companionship and mutual assistance, our hearts set on a quest, patient and light-hearted about the little mishaps — misplaced blankets, weary limbs and tea-stained maps. Today's troubles pale into insignificance as the sun's rays reflect a glimmer of glory on the horizon — maybe tomorrow in new Jerusalem!

If we hope to travel into tomorrow, we must be able to move on. We cannot allow our yesterdays to be heavy, useless, excess baggage. They must become living memories of the many blessings and joys life has given. Memory can be an act of faith: looking back we find that tragedy and loss were also special opportunities, moments of grace. In the wilderness, even in the midst of treachery and rejection, God "tended us... guided us" (Psalm 77 [78]:72)[1].

Just as we survived past difficulties, we learn not to lose hope in the present moment. God took care of us before, so now we trust that we will find the right path, make the right decision. "You are always with me; you hold me by the right hand. You guide me with your counsel and lead me to glory" (Psalm 72 [73]:23-24).

Trusting the present moment means accepting today as a present, a gift, which is all the more special because tomorrow it will be gone. The eyes of the traveller learn to see and the limbs of the wayfarer to appreciate all that life offers — mountains and valleys, storms and flowers. "O God, the eyes of all look on you with hope. You give us food, your hand is open wide, you fill all things with your blessings" (Psalm 144 [145]:15-16).

The faith we have learned from yesterday, the trust we have in the present, make us confidently practical about tomorrow. How do we want the journey to end? Do we know where we are headed? Are there stops along the way we want to make but keep postponing? Sustained by yesterday's treasured memories, encouraged by the blessings and love we now enjoy, we have the courage to plan for tomorrow. "His hand shall lead me, his right hand shall hold on to me" (Psalm 138 [139]:10).

Companion on Life's Journey hopes to offer something for every traveller: the young and the old; the weary and tired, as well as those rejoicing in their strength and good fortunes; those whose journey has been long and eventful, and those who are only recently aware of how life is a venture in learning again and again to say goodby and hello.

Chapter 1, "Signs for Recognizing the Way to God," reflects on how the sacraments are signs for life's journey: signs pointing out that God is with us on our pilgrimage. Perhaps nothing so much as travelling reminds us of the importance of the simple things of life: water, bread, wine, companions, tears, an embrace, a hand to hold. These simple ordinary things become in the sacraments our experience of the Kingdom of God.

Similarly, the fragmentary moment we call now, the come-again-gone-again rhythm of seasons, becomes through faith our discovery of eternity. The Church's celebration of the sacramental mystery of time is known as the liturgical year: the yearly cycle of reflection, repentance and renewal manifested in Lent-Easter-Pentecost and reflected in Advent-Christmas-Epiphany.

The short meditations on the sacraments and the liturgical year have been chosen in light of their ongoing reality. Sacramental reality is never finished and done with but lives on in us, revealing the depths of God's Good News: the Kingdom is already in our midst and yet is still to come in fullness.

Chapter 2, "Daily Guide for God's People in Prayer," outlines a week of morning and evening prayer in the tradition of the Church's daily office of prayer. Just as we celebrate and consecrate life year by year through the liturgical seasons, so also each day reflects our journey in faith: being born in hope each morning, accepting with trust and love sunset and evening rest. Morning and evening, life and death, are the pattern which gives shape and rhythm to prayer. This pattern is shared by all God's creatures — and over the centuries has inspired Jews and Christians to join the Psalmist in offering prayer to God at daybreak (Psalm 5:3) and singing God's song at night (Psalm 41 [42]:8).

Chapter 3, "Milestones of Faith and Moments for Prayer," is a collection of many devotions familiar to older Catholics. These prayers are included partly to meet the needs of those whose spirit yearns to hear a familiar word from the past, and partly to serve as reminders of our faith's journey. Prayers and devotions change with the times; what is popular in one decade might not serve the needs of another. Nevertheless, these familiar milestones are witnesses to the faith of those who have gone before us and also of our own personal pilgrimage: where we have come from, the blessings of yesterday which have made us who we are today.

Recognizing that the Christian enjoys the liberty and bounty of God's Spirit, the Church provides a variety of prayers and devotions from many ages and cultures. We are free to take from the Church's treasury what is helpful and compatible with our own needs, all the time remembering that human words and devotions are but shadows of the full reality — no eye fully sees, no ear really comprehends, no human heart fully grasps what God is doing (1 Corinthians 2:9).

Chapter 4, "Readings and Meditations for the Wayfarer," like the prayers and devotions of Chapter 3, represents various perspectives and traditions. They have been chosen with basically one underlying theme: that we are finite, mortal beings, every day growing older. Such is the wonder of the human mystery: God's glory embraces mortal flesh, eternal wisdom is revealed in the apparent folly of passing time, and the Immortal One speaks to us through human words. No matter how old we may be, growing older is a challenge we all share. The experiences and insights of others can assist each of us as we journey onward into life.

Note

[1] Psalms throughout this book are cited according to both the traditional and contemporary numbering found in Bibles. The first reference is to the numbering traditionally common to Catholic editions of the Bible; the second reference is to the numbering used in Protestant and ecumenical editions.

1

Signs for Recognizing the Way to God

Baptism: Dying and Rising in Christ

You do remember that we who have been baptized into Jesus Christ have been baptized into his death? By being baptized into his death, we were buried with him so that just as the Father's glory raised Christ from the dead, so also we might walk in new life. For as we have been united with him in death, we shall be one with him in resurrection.

Romans 6:4-5

FOLLOWING CHRIST'S PATTERN

Conversion and repentance are not one-time actions; they are a way of life. Moreover, they are to be my way of life. It is not enough to rest on the past commitment of baptism; I must renew my conversion daily.

Christian life is, quite simply, a demanding vocation — one that constantly asks us to "think better" of our goals, motives and lifestyles. Our model for this rethinking is also our model for action, Christ Jesus. We are to pattern our thought, our fundamental direction, on his life-giving emptying of self.

Father Kenneth Pearce, *Living with Christ*

A DAILY CHOICE

The choice between Gospel and possessions, Jesus and myself, is the very thing that we have decided by baptism and reaffirmed each Easter. Baptism states that we have decided that nothing will be permitted to come between us and the Gospel, ourselves and the Lord.

The demands of the Gospel are to be lived out within the great choice of our past, within baptism. They are also to be heard and lived in the simple actions of life. Thus the "death to sin and alive for Christ" aspect of baptism becomes the "cup of cold water given to the little one" whom we meet each day. Baptism becomes a daily gesture of hospitality.

Father Kenneth Pearce, *Living with Christ*

Confirmation: Anointed and Strengthened in Christ

You have been anointed by the Holy One. Let what you heard in the beginning continue to live in you, and as long as what you heard lives in you, you will live in the Son and in the Father. This is what he promises: everlasting life. His anointing lives in you, teaching you everything in truth. Live in Christ, my children.

1 John 2:20, 24-25, 27

STRENGTHENING ONE ANOTHER

Picture a tired Moses being helped to remain in a posture of prayer, with Aaron and Hur at his side (Exodus 17:8-13). Let Moses be a symbol for yourself, and let Aaron and Hur represent those believers around you.

Our lives cannot be lived in isolation. Each of us is part of the community of Christ. For us to grow, to live and to face challenges like Moses, we need the support of our fellow believers. And the community (you and I) is meant to provide it.

Each of us also needs to play the part of Aaron and Hur... to confirm our neighbors in faith. We need to comfort someone experiencing tragedy to bring a community of consolation to him. We need to understand and to stay with someone who is having doubts of faith to bring the community to hold up that person's arms in faith. We need to refuse to judge another and thus to say that believers are not against him but with him. And when we do so, we are like Aaron and Hur supporting a tired Moses.

Richard P. Hardy, *Living with Christ*

ANOINTED WITH CHRIST'S SIGN

The death of Jesus and its meaning reflected in the symbol of the cross is something like a work of art. It stands there waiting to be probed, interpreted and absorbed.

We press the cross into the forehead of persons preparing for baptism. Even infants are "signed" by their parents, godparents and pastor. Christians are "sealed" with the cross in confirmation, and feel the oil of chrism rubbed into their skin.

We have different ways of marking the cross on our bodies when we begin to pray and when we prepare to hear the Gospel.

We kiss the cross as a sign of our love and reverence for its meaning and its power.

Let these gestures be a deep and sincere "yes" to the Christ who invites us to live and die and live in him.

Father Corbin Eddy, *Living with Christ*

Eucharist:
Christ Lives in Us

I have been crucified with Christ. I no longer live; it is Christ who lives in me. The life I now live in the flesh I live by faith: faith in the Son of God who loved me and gave himself for me.

Galatians 2:20

TRANSFORMED IN CHRIST

In every Eucharist we offer to God the bread and wine that "earth has given and human hands have made." This offering is a symbol of our whole lives. Because of Christ, who also worked "with human hands," our offering is accepted, transformed and given back to us as a "share in his divinity."

There should be no split between our worship and our workaday lives, for through the Mass, our work, offered to God and transformed into his life, becomes a leaven for our whole environment. Christ's goal is to restore the whole world to its Creator. Then his work will be complete.

Lettie Morse, *Living with Christ*

OUR AMEN IS A HUMBLE YES

In the bread broken and the cup shared, Jesus surrenders himself to those who accept him in faith. He becomes for us food and drink, transforming us into himself, giving us strength to say "yes," to follow him and to "pass from this world to the Father."

Our "yes" is to be lived out in humble service and in Eucharist... like washing feet and giving Eucharistic thanks.

Father Barry McGrory, *Living with Christ*

THE GIVER IS THE GIFT

The Eucharistic meal — the Body and Blood of the Lord — is the gift. Jesus is the giver. In truth the giver is the gift...

Over each lifetime he gives you and me the inner light and strength to move — slowly almost always, and sometimes painfully — toward that liberation and fullness promised all believers. He asks in return only that we open ourselves with childlike faith and trust to the gift of himself.

Grant Maxwell, *Living with Christ*

Reconciliation: Forgiven and Forgiving

If one of you trespasses, the spiritual among you should restore that person in a spirit of gentleness, not forgetting that any of you may be tempted. You should bear each other's burdens and thus fulfil Christ's law. Examine your own conduct. Do not think you can deceive God: what you sow, you will reap.

Galatians 6:1-2, 7

WE ARE THE WORK OF HIS HANDS

Repentance is woven into the warp and woof of the fabric of our lives.

To be repentant is to experience God's holiness and love, and to experience our self in the light of that encounter. We see what we are, what we are not, what we can be.

His gentle, still voice calls, "I have Good News for you. Come and listen to it." Listen to his message of love, encouragement, his offer to help us sort out the various strands we're weaving into our life pattern. Some threads we'll keep, some we'll discard (we learn from our mistakes too!)

His is an offer we shouldn't refuse. He is not only the pattern, he is the master weaver. With his help, our lives can take on a

new, richer texture, and we can admire his-and-our handiwork together.

Mary Landry, *Living with Christ*

LOVE FORGIVES

Jesus' pardon of the woman with the "bad name" is a heart-warming example of the Lord's liberating forgiveness. Jesus does not say that the woman's loving acts of gratitude earn her God's forgiveness. Rather he says that her generous gestures show that she has been freed from sin by the miracles of repentance and divine pardon.

The Lord also points out that where little has been forgiven, little love is evident.

Each day you and I pray to the Father to "forgive us our trespasses as we forgive those who trespass against us." We commit ourselves before God to forgive one another as we are forgiven through Jesus. We promise to struggle against the resentment we often feel when wronged, to forgo revenge, to forgive instead.

The continuing miracle of reconciliation is possible only through persisting faith — our utter trust in the liberating power and compassion of Jesus. Time after time he forgives us and sets us free to love again.

Grant Maxwell, *Living with Christ*

Marriage: Witnessing to Love

Imitate God as his beloved children. Follow the way of Christ, walking in his love who gave himself up for us. No one hates his body but rather cherishes and nourishes it, just as Christ treats the Church, because it is his body and we are its members. "This is why a man shall leave father and mother and be joined to his wife, and the two become one body." This great mystery I understand to apply to Christ and his Church, and so you too should love your wives as yourselves and a wife should respect her husband.

Ephesians 5:1-2, 29-33

SHARING THE JOURNEY

Most of us usually like to travel with family members or friends, although sometimes we may want to travel on our own. Chances are, however, that we would soon feel rootless, even afraid, if we had to spend a lifetime travelling alone.

Christian living is a lifelong journey toward our eternal home. This pilgrimage of faith never was intended to mean "doing your own thing" in isolation from other believers. It's meant to be a shared experience, from baptism to our final committal to God's mercy.

Grant Maxwell, *Living with Christ*

INTIMACY GIVES LIFE MEANING

Most couples know that they can't draw a road map for their marriage. If lovers ask each other, "What will your love do for me?" they have no answer except "I will be there for you." They can only hope to have a deep sense of intimacy and care, which will be nourished and expressed in different ways throughout their marriage.

It is like that with God and us. We do not know the many ways he will express his love for us, or what that love will lead us to do for him. It will take various forms in our lives, inviting us into experiences we had not anticipated. At times, he will call us to be with him in situations that are difficult and threatening. It was that way with the prophets; it was so with Jesus.

However, he asks us to share our lives with him — at the center of it all will be a deep sense of his intimacy and care. Nothing we do will be more important than sharing this tenderness. Nothing we do will be worthwhile if we lose this sense of intimacy. It nourishes and gives meaning to all we do.

Marriage can be scary; so can God's love. Lovers choose that commitment because, in the end, it is a freeing, joyful experience in which they know they are special. We commit ourselves to God because he loves us. In that love, we know we are someone special.

Father Richard Shields, OFM Conv.,
Living with Christ

RESPONDING IN LOVE

Christian marriage is a sign of the union between Christ and his Church. Our unity as the family of God results from the "marriage" of Christ with his Church. We are to be one, united in Christ by his Spirit. Jesus is the reason for our unity as Church. Through his sufferings and death he has identified us with himself and has become the brother and leader of all the sons and daughters of God. We are all called to respond.

Anne and Pete remember the forty years of married life stored in their consciousness — memories of bringing five children into the world, the sickness, the upsets, the joys, the celebrations that mark the experience of any family memory.

Tom and Betty are a couple engaged to be married in a few weeks' time, with all the dreams and hopes for their future together, coupled with the last-minute arrangements that still need to be settled before their wedding day.

Brian is a single parent, divorced from his wife and faced with the responsibility of being both mother and father to his two young children. Susan is also a single parent with a young daughter but she has never married; she is among the growing number of women who choose to have children but who choose not to be married.

Sister Anne's final vows of chastity, poverty and obedience, proclaimed just a month ago, still ring in her ears, and Father Joe has thirty years of celibate priesthood in his memory. Steven's celibacy has been for ten years, ever since his beloved wife died of cancer; and Nancy is a woman who has made a deliberate choice of a non-vowed single life.

How do you and I respond? Whatever our situation in life we are called to be in loving relationship with others — our families, the people with whom we work, the friends with whom we socialize. Whatever our lifestyle may be, we are expected to share a covenant of love with others, in good times and in bad, reaching out to

others with the love with which Jesus loved his disciples... a close companionship developed through a relationship with others as unique persons. Whatever our situation in life, whatever our lifestyle and whatever our memories may be, this is certainly an exciting challenge to us all.

Alex Campbell, *Living with Christ*

Holy Orders: Ministering to Others' Needs

There is a variety of gifts but the same Spirit. There is a variety of service but the same Lord. There is a variety of work but the same God who inspires them. The Spirit is given to each for the common good. You together are Christ's body and individually its members.

1 Corinthians 12:4-7, 27

EXPRESSIONS OF JESUS AMONG US

It was the need for some tangible expression of the Father's love which prompted Jesus to give other people a share in his mission. He appointed apostles to announce that the Kingdom of God was among us, and to demonstrate that presence through healing and answering the needs of the oppressed and neglected.

By giving to others a share in his mission, he was telling us that it is the responsibility of every Christian to respond to need, realizing that in so doing we are, in God's own mysterious way, vehicles through which the Father's love reaches others.

In our community of believers today, the fulfilment of some needs has been formalized and given the name "ministry." While it is necessary to organize things so that certain essential needs are fulfilled, none of us can presume that the Church, as institution, is capable of satisfying them all through her ministries. It therefore becomes necessary for each of us to be sensitive to the changing needs of people around us and to use our talents creatively in the service of others. In doing so after the manner of Jesus, we become part of his continuing presence among us.

Father James Casper, SCJ, *Living with Christ*

FOLLOWING, GIVING, SERVING

Shepherds in Jesus' day did not wear snow-white robes and stand around with cuddly lambs in their arms. They were the simplest and poorest of folk who lived a very rough life while performing an important service for the community.

When Jesus said, "I am the good shepherd," he was applying to himself many good qualities which shepherds had and which the Good Shepherd Gospel suggests: sensitivity, courage, generosity and gentleness, patience and self-denial.

Jesus' values are simple, not fancy. His option is for the poor. What would he say today? "I am the good cleaning lady; I am

the good postman; I am the good typist; I am the good farmworker..."

May the familiar and yet unexpected voice of the Good Shepherd call each of us to follow, to give and to serve.

Father Michael Czerny, SJ, *Living with Christ*

Anointing of the Sick: Healing in Christ

Is any among you suffering? Let that person pray. If someone is rejoicing, let that person sing a song of praise. Is someone among you sick? Let that person call for the elders of the Church; let them pray over and anoint the sick person with oil in the name of the Lord. The prayer of faith will save the sick person and the Lord will raise that person up; if there are sins which have been committed, they will be forgiven. So confess your sins to one another and pray for one another, and you will be healed. The prayer of the righteous is powerful.

James 5:13-16

EMBRACING OUR HUMANITY

When we pray for healing, what exactly is our hope? That we will be rid of a cancer, a great debt of injustice, or even a wayward son or daughter? Somehow at the heart of all our prayer it seems we desire to be removed from our circumstances.

Perhaps that is why we are often so dissatisfied with the answer to our prayer — which seems like no answer. So often the answer leads us to assimilate our pain or our problems, enabling us to accept these in a new way, that is, as part of the human family, enriching our relationships and restoring us as life-giving and healing members of the community.

Jesus in the Gospel not only declares his desire to heal but appears to be especially concerned that we understand the meaning of his healing. His desire to heal is a desire to fully embrace man's condition as weak, as sinner. His desire is to heal us with an inner healing of the heart that must overflow into building community.

His answer to our prayer is for a growing concern with our suffering brothers and sisters, with their injustice. He desires that we rediscover our wayward sons, daughters, husbands... He doesn't permit us to disown our humanity.

Father Robert Nagy, *Living with Christ*

SAFE IN GOD'S EMBRACE

Our faith in the resurrection does not have to do with something which is totally divorced from our present life. It is rather the unfolding of our trust in a life-giving and faithful God. We believe that we are loved, embraced and cared for by a gracious God. And we trust that even death cannot put an end to this love, embrace and care.

We are like the child who lives under the good care of his mother. He takes it for granted each night that she will be there to care for him in the morning. We are confident that the God of Jesus will not let go of us. We shall be safe.

Father William Marrevee, SCJ,
Living with Christ

COME FORTH AND LIVE!

On one occasion, felled by a serious illness, past fighting for my own life, I was unable to sense the presence or the reality of God or even to ask for help. I needed someone to come to me. And someone did come, a Sister who asked simply, "Do you want to be anointed?"

In that anointing, someone came indeed and I knew resurrection to new life, felt it with joy in my bones. I can never forget. It was resurrection in December. The medics and others recognized that I had been brought back to life. "What happened?" they asked me.

When someone comes and calls us to life — calls us by name: Mary, John, Joe, Helen — it is the hour to answer. It is our chance to live. Like Lazarus responding to that strong voice, we get up, step out, and are freed from the winding sheets, the bindings that keep us in a state of more or less "rigor mortis."

What is this new life to which we are called? It is a shift from being sunk in the self, to being grandly activated by the living Spirit. It is living the life that is larger than life, the project of Jesus Christ with us in this world. He offers us life and gives us his Spirit as the promise that it will last. We need never again fear that we are not worth it, or that our little life will be snuffed out as if it didn't matter. We were called by name in baptism and given the Spirit to confirm life in us. Come forth.

Sister Mary Alban Bouchard, CSJ,
Living with Christ

Liturgical Year: Seeing Christ in Time

Even if this is an evil age, make the most of time. Be filled with the Spirit. Sing psalms and hymns, praising and singing to the Lord with all your heart, so that in all seasons and for all things you are giving thanks to God our Father in the name of our Lord Jesus Christ.

Ephesians 5:16, 18-20

CHURCH YEAR

The Church calendar heals. It invites us to face (not run away from) our emptiness, our need for redemption. Then we reflect on our fullness, the gift of God already begun.

For it is not possible to savor and assimilate in a single day the mystery Paul speaks of: God cares enough to become one of us; one with all of us and each of us.

Father Barry McGrory, *Living with Christ*

We celebrate all the "mysteries" or events of Jesus' life one by one through the liturgical year, the better to gently savor them, to grasp more completely each facet of his life so as to relate it to our own personal struggle. Each of these mysteries has its own proper gift and shapes us slowly according to its own prayer form. So Jesus' birth rejoices us, his baptism dignifies us, his passion heals us. The particular fruit which matures year by year can marvelously vary in accordance with our own situation.

But Easter towers over the other feasts. For forty days we prepare to renew in earnest our baptismal vows. Then, far from lapsing back, we celebrate our new freedom in the Lord for fifty days.

Father Barry McGrory, *Living with Christ*

CHRISTMAS

God's way of loving us is so specific. There is a little baby, the first-born, and there is the on-going process of God's love unfolding in the simplest of all images, the family that receives the baby.

The incarnation, God with us, is an ongoing communion between God and people. There's give and take in love. We accept God's love in accepting the baby. And God receives our love, which is very concrete.

Our way of loving is seen in the image of Mary and Joseph meeting the baby's simple but constant needs, attending to the religious requirements by going to the Temple for purification after the birth, listening to people's praise and their warnings that were offered. As well as an image of the human community accepting God's love, the image of the Holy Family is an image of God accepting love as helplessly as a newborn. It is an image that affirms our way of living.

Mary, Joseph and Jesus were involved in the process of love, and call our attention to our own processes of love within our families and the Christian community — to everyday manifestations of love. There are joyous moments, such as Simeon proclaims, "My eyes have seen the salvation you promised," and there are grave disappointments, the sword that will pierce Mary's soul (Luke 2:30, 35). But mostly there are in-between times. There are meals to prepare and children's noses to wipe. This is "God with us" too.

Roberta Morris, *Living with Christ*

EPIPHANY

At Christmas we celebrate that God's Word became flesh and dwelt among us. The phrase really means "he has pitched his tent among us." The visit of the Savior is not a passing one, but it is to last for as long as humanity makes its pilgrimage through this world. Jesus does not rely on the externals of power and influence to proclaim his presence now any more than he did at the beginning. He does rely on people who, like those wise men from the East, catch the significance of that presence, rejoice in it and proclaim it boldly.

Epiphany says: Jesus has come for all, but it also says: The effects of his coming are not automatic. The believer is one who accepts that God can still surprise, one who is ready to "hitch his or her wagon" to the divine star rather than to another, one who rejoices in living for the moment when the Messiah is clearly seen and when it is at last understood where and why God's star was leading.

J. Kevin Coyle, *Living with Christ*

ADVENT

Who are the ones who "seek the face of God"? They are the people who expect and desire God's presence. Those who seek are those who will have their eyes open and therefore those who will see. Those who seek are those who find. They see and recognize the face of God in the signs of his acting presence among us.

Far from putting God to the test to give proofs, they are the ones who believe he comes today and so are sensitive to his presence. They find him in the new life that is everywhere. They find him in the world of nature when spring comes out of winter. They find him in human life when growth comes out of suffering. They find him in the Church, sinful yet life-giving in its sacraments and community. They find him in every new life, every child who "comes with the message that God is not yet discouraged of man" (Rabindranath Tagore).

Like Mary, they are already expecting and waiting when the message comes that he is here. A daring faith and an open heart will recognize the signs and receive the Coming One, the expected Jesus. Everyone who seeks the face of God is like a virgin ready to let Jesus be conceived and formed within and then revealed to the world.

The one who truly seeks the face of God also desires that his face be seen by others. Every Christian is called to believe the sign of God-with-us in Christ and then is missioned to preach by his or her very life the Good News... God has come... he is here... and he is still coming.

The one who sees becomes the sign; the sinner becomes the saint: God's beloved in Rome, Toronto, Tokyo...

Sister Mary Alban Bouchard, CSJ,
Living with Christ

BAPTISM OF CHRIST

Somehow, children seem to enjoy surprises so much more so than adults. Perhaps children have a simple openness to life which allows them to be surprised, whereas adults are preoccupied with planning life. Of course, once we have invested time and energy into planning, we do not give up our plans easily, and so we leave little room for surprises. These always force us to reconsider.

Yet our God has shown us time and again that he is a God of surprises. He surprised the people who were so sure that John the Baptist was the promised man-of-God who would deliver Israel. But instead of John, who lived in the tradition of the great men of God, God showed that his Chosen One was an ordinary man, Jesus, who was so much like them that the people took no notice of him. He was so much a part of them that he presented himself to be baptized by John as they did. At that point he seemed to portray few characteristics of the great prophets or the expected deliverer.

Somehow, like these people, we keep expecting to see God in extraordinary people or settings, and we hold on to strict rules, about when and where and under what conditions we will encounter God. We won't allow God to surprise us, and so we miss him.

When we come to terms with the truth that God is present in what is ordinary, perhaps we will then allow him to surprise us. And how he can surprise us at times by allowing his simple truths to be spoken by a child, or by revealing his understanding love in the warm memories of an aged grandparent.

Father James Casper, SCJ, *Living with Christ*

LENT

God's strange command to Abraham to "leave the land I will show you" (Genesis 12:1) rings again in our reluctant ears. It is a kind of theme for living... and for Lent.

Most of us are not eager to hear that message. Since there seems to be a lot of instability around us already, we would feel much better with a word of consolation, a word which would invite us to come nearer rather than to go far away!

But half-heartedly we go. Slowly we climb again that familiar ramp onto the moving highway.

Lent is a journey which makes special demands on each of us... just like the Lord's command to Abraham. It challenges us to discover not only what we should take for the road but also what we can expect to find on it.

What indeed is needed and what can we expect to find? We need a lot of trust: in someone or something. Reliable guides or at least maps are essential from the outset. We must travel light, leave behind whatever will slow us down. We need refreshment along the way... essentials such as water to quench our thirst. We must be able to see and to know what to look for on the road. We need an expectancy and motivation which will carry us beyond the sufferings of the moment and give us the courage to go on to our destination.

As we journey from Sunday to Sunday on our lenten travels, let's keep a watchful eye open for these five signs by the roadside. As we glance at them, in passing by, may they remind us again that we need not be half-hearted for the journey since we can indeed travel meaningfully. May they also fill us with that confidence which comes with knowing how to get there!

Jerome Herauf, *Living with Christ*

HOLY WEEK

Every day of Holy Week is a day for reenacting and remembering. We gather for our week-long experience of returning to the beginning.

The beginning of our story as a community of believing people, as Church, lies in the story of Jesus' suffering and death for us and his resurrection.

When we hear the Passion, we are hearing the story of our roots. It is the story of a God who loved us, and made himself vulnerable by becoming one of us, even to allowing himself to be destroyed by death as we are. And when he gave us all that he had, the Father raised him from death and, with him, the Father also raises us.

Because we are all contained in him and in his love, his story is our story too.

Father James Casper, SCJ, *Living with Christ*

EASTER VIGIL

There's a story told of Saint Francis and his monks that might help us enter more freely into the Easter Vigil. It seems there was a time that Francis told his brothers they were going into town and preach. So they went to the town square. Francis and the brothers walked around the square silently greeting those they met and continued this until dark. In exasperation, one of his brothers asked, "When do we preach?" And Francis answered, "We have."

The vigil is that kind of celebration. It is a sermon in itself. It is a walking through our history and our story of salvation. In the remembering, the telling, the walking and the singing we are refurbished. All those parts of our journey are seen again in a new way, owned again in a new way, reaffirmed and proclaimed again in a new way. The vigil, the oldest of our celebrations of the Christian mystery of Jesus' death and resurrection, calls us into the darkness and void of death and sin so that, with Jesus, we will look forward to journeying in faith, to a new way of being alive beyond the tragedy of death — Jesus' and our own.

Waiting in darkness for the birth of light, by the glimmer we journey to grasp and expand the light as it comes to us from each other, from our own stories and those of the prophets.

The history of salvation is every person's history and so we receive in baptism all those who wish to join us on that journey, meanwhile joyfully recalling all those who peopled and blessed that journey before us across the sea of life and death. We remember in the Eucharist that we are a people rooted and alive in all people and events of the past and those still to come. We are on a journey in faith by which we are fully incorporated through Jesus in the Godhead, from whence we came. We taste and see... we eat and drink... how good is the Lord.

Robert Nagy, *Living with Christ*

EASTER

If we read or listen to the passion of Jesus simply as a story of a past event, forever gone and finished, then we are mere spectators to a sad, unjust and tragic event in which a just and good man loses — as is so often the case even today.

But Jesus' death and resurrection gives us a different message. It invites us to enter triumphantly with Jesus into victory over evil, oppression and injustice — to experience the victorious power of the Kingdom.

We are not recalling just a past event but entering our own personal passion, our struggle in union with Jesus our brother and victorious Messiah. We experience the suffering-death-resurrection tension in our own lives. We struggle along with Jesus to rid ourselves of our selfishness, our slavery to sin, to experience the victory of the resurrection, which is freedom over selfishness, injustice and interior emptiness.

To follow Jesus, our triumphant Messiah, is always a paradox. He tells us that in order to win, we must know how to lose: "for whoever wants to save his life will lose it; but whoever loses his life for me and the Gospel will save it" (Mark 8:35).

This paradox is part of everyone's life: without struggle there is no victory. If an athlete experiences only the overwhelming of his opponent, he does not really appreciate the victory. Only if he participates in a real struggle does the victory become really meaningful.

It is the same with the victory that the Church, the People of God, experiences through participating in the passion struggle. We, the messianic people, along with the triumphant Messiah, Jesus, celebrate a victory... a resurrection victory.

Father Tim Amyot, OSM, *Living with Christ*

ASCENSION

The Ascension evokes the image of Jesus leaving us. The truth is that it says more about his choice to stay with us. In order to stay he had to leave.

We know the painful experience of letting go: of a child, a parent, a friend, a lover... We let go because we know we must. To hold on would be not to hold care-fully. To tighten our grasp would be to warp wings that must fly, wings readied even by our own care. We let go and can only trust ourselves to keep on living. Perhaps the flight will not be long? or too far away?

God asks us to let go of him again and again. His "leaving" us is his longing to be more himself with us, his offer to us to be more ourselves, but the time "in between" feels like a time without him. The Ascension affirms that he is never more present than when he seems to be absent.

It is a time when we may see only one pair of footprints on the shores of life. It is a lonely time. Then, someday, we come to see again. We look back and know: we were being carried then.

It is a time when God trusts us enough to slip out of our sight, to penetrate deep within our hearts, and from there invites us to greater strength and courage — to faith-full-ness. And we discover God where we least suspect him to be — within ourselves. "He departed from our sight, that we might return to our heart and there find him" (Saint Augustine).

If we can find him in our own hearts, perhaps we can let ourselves discover him in every person of every culture and country — even in those we have proclaimed "God-forsaken."

Sister Rosemary Brosseau, CND,
Living with Christ

PENTECOST

Pentecost — the birthday of the Church, the moment when the Church takes consciousness of itself. In turn, each of us must ask the question: what is the Church? what am I doing in the Church, for the Church?

The Church is the community of love whose members are filled with the Holy Spirit and called to reach out to all people. This dynamic community is formed of men and women who seek to grow one with the other and to learn from one another. It is the Spirit that inspires each of us to reach out, to listen, to learn from the other. This

other-oriented attitude will lead us to the peace that Jesus assures us will fill our lives.

At Pentecost Jesus sends his Church. He gives us a living fire that burns within each one of us. He sends us to bring greater harmony into our society. Our concern for justice for everyone must spread the warmth of the Father's love and the Son's life. In this way, the Church will witness love and seek to bring greater unity and purpose to our world.

The Spirit that came to the early Church comes to us today. The unity and singleness of mind of that initial Pentecost can exist today if we stay open to the gifts that the Spirit brings. For these gifts never fade. Our role in the daily Pentecost of the Church is to constantly strive to reach out, to listen to others' needs and to voice concern, to receive others' gifts as we share our own.

Maurice Charbonneau, *Living with Christ*

ORDINARY TIME

For many centuries the Hebrew people had no written word of the Scriptures to tell them about God but they were still able to hear his word to them. They had a faith

vision of reality whereby they recognized God's presence and heard his voice calling to them in all the events and circumstances of their daily existence. In all of this, the call of God to them was present, and they knew they had to respond to that call; they knew they had to decide, one way or another.

This faith vision of reality is summed up beautifully in a delightful verse of Elizabeth Barrett Browning:

Earth's crammed with heaven
And every common bush afire with God
But only he who sees takes off his shoes
The rest just sit around and pluck blackberries.

As with the Old Testament people of God, so too with each of us. God continues to speak to us and call us in all our daily situations and events. The point is, though, do we see this presence and recognize him? Do we take off our shoes in reverence? Or do we sit around, uninterested and unrecognizing as we busy ourselves with picking blackberries?

Alex Campbell, *Living with Christ*

Have you ever reflected on the power of "little" things? It is amazing how something quite small can affect a person's well-being... the "mighty" mosquito!... the "little things" which "mean a lot," "get you down" or "count."

Jesus appreciated the paradoxical power of "little things" when he used the image of the mustard seed to teach his disciples a lesson about faith. But, as is so often the case with metaphors, Jesus wants to lead us beyond the image. When the disciples request an "increase" in faith, it is obvious to Jesus they have not yet realized that, concerning faith, there is no such thing as "more" or "less."

Faith is a gift. In the realm of God's gifts there is no such thing as a scale of measurement. Size and quantity simply do not merit consideration. What is important is our simple believing that God desires to give all that is needed. All faith is "enough" faith because it is the doing of God and not of ourselves.

Sister Mary Ann Hinsdale, IHM,
Living with Christ

2

Daily Guide for God's People in Prayer

Sunday
Morning Prayer

CALL TO PRAYER

Let our hearts be ready for the Lord Jesus. Let us welcome him whose glory and power endures for all ages.

HYMN

The Spirit cries:
This is the paschal feast,
the Lord's Passover.

Lord Jesus,
you protect us from disaster,
your arms over us in fatherly protection,
wings sheltering us like a mother bird.
Because you love us,
you turned eternal wrath from us,
giving us eternal friendship.

This is the feast of the Spirit,
a mystic dance for every day of the year.
All creatures delight and rejoice;
death has been destroyed, life restored.
God is revealed as human,
and humanity has gone up as God
while the earth sings and dances.

Adapted from an Easter hymn
by Hippolytus of Rome (died 235)

PSALM 8

Lord our God,
your name is great through all the earth.

Your majesty is praised above the heavens
by the lips of children and infants.
Yet the firmament you established
quiets those who rebel against you.

I look at the heavens, the work of your hands,
the moon and stars you set in place —
what are we that you should be mindful of us,
that you care for the children of humanity?

You have made us little less than gods,
you crown us with splendor and honor,
making us rulers over your handiwork,
setting all things beneath our feet:
sheep and cattle, the wild beasts,
the birds of the air, the fish of the sea,
everything that travels the ocean paths.

Lord our God,
your name is great through all the earth.

PSALM 97 (98)

Sing a new song to the Lord
for he does wonderful things.
His right hand, his holy arm,
has the power to save.

The Lord shows forth his might,
he reveals his justice to all nations.
He remembers his mercy and loving
  kindness
for the house of Israel.

The ends of the earth
see God's wonderful deeds.
Shout with joy, all the earth,
sing to the Lord.

Take harps and instruments,
horns and trumpets,
proclaim triumphantly:
God is King!

Let the ocean and its deeps applaud,
the world and its creatures;
let the rivers clap with glee
and the mountains echo in joy.

For the Lord comes —
to judge the earth with his justice,
to rule over the world and its peoples
in righteousness.

READING

God said, "Here is the sign of the covenant I am making between myself and you and every living creature among you for all generations. I am setting my rainbow in the clouds and it shall be a sign of the covenant between me and the earth. When I gather the clouds of the heavens over the earth and the rainbow appears in the clouds, I will remember the covenant between me and you and every living creature of every kind. And so the waters shall never again become a flood to destroy all creatures of flesh. When the rainbow is in the clouds, I shall see it and remember my covenant."

Genesis 9:12-15

CANTICLE

Blessed be the Lord, the God of Israel.
He has visited his people,
coming to their rescue.

He has raised up for us a power for
 salvation
in the house of his servant David —
just as he proclaimed
through his holy prophets from ancient
 times,
that he would save us from our enemies
and from the hands of all who hate us.

Thus he shows mercy to our ancestors,
remembering his holy covenant,
the oath he swore to our father Abraham,
that he would grant us, free from fear,
to be delivered from our enemies,

to serve him in holiness and righteousness,
in his presence, all our days.

And you, little child, shall be called
prophet of the Most High,
for you will go before the Lord,
preparing the way before him;

giving his people knowledge of salvation
through the forgiveness of their sins,
in the tender mercy of our God;

bringing to us from on high the rising sun,
giving light to those who live in darkness
and the shadow of death;
guiding our feet
into the way of peace.

"Benedictus," Luke 1:68-79

INTERCESSIONS

May God give the Church love and hope: Lord, we trust in your mercy.

May God give the world peace and justice: Lord, we trust in your mercy.

May God give the sick and the suffering comfort and strength: Lord, we trust in your mercy.

May God give light and grace to my family and friends: Lord, we trust in your mercy.

Our Father...

BLESSING

We are God's beloved, called to be saints. May God our Father and the Lord Jesus Christ send us grace and peace. Amen.

Evening Prayer

CALL TO PRAYER

Holy, holy, holy is the Lord, God the Almighty, who was, and is, and still is to come. With joy let us praise Father, Son and Holy Spirit.

HYMN

You are the light that brings joy,
the glory of the immortal Father.
Jesus Christ, holy and blessed,
the sun is setting,
evening lights begin to shine.

With you, in your Spirit,
we praise the Father
because of the light you have given us,
Son of God, giver of life.
At all times we sing your praise
and the earth acclaims your glory.

"Phos hilaron," Byzantine vesper hymn

PSALM 83 (84)

How lovely is your dwelling place,
Lord, God of hosts.

My soul longs and yearns
to enter the house of the Lord;
my heart and flesh sing for joy
to the living God.

The sparrow finds a home,
the swallow a nest for her young,
at your altar, Lord of hosts,
my King, my God.

Blessed are they who dwell in your house,
singing your praise all day long.
Blessed are those inspired by you —
in their hearts are the roads to Zion.

As they go through the valley of dryness,
they find it a place of springs,
blessed by autumn rains.
They make their way from height to height,
for God appears to them in Zion.

Lord, God of hosts, hear my prayer,
listen to me, God of Jacob.
God, our protector,
look on the face of your anointed.

One day in your house
is better than a thousand elsewhere;
to stand at the door of the house of the Lord

is better than living in the tents of the
ungodly.

For God is our shelter and shield.
The Lord gives favor and honor,
withholding nothing good
from those who walk in innocence.

Lord of hosts,
happy they who trust in you.

PSALM 66 (67)

May God be gracious to us and bless us;
may his face shine upon us.

Let your way be known upon the earth,
your saving power among all peoples.

Let the peoples praise you, Lord,
let all the peoples praise you.

Let the nations be glad and rejoice —
for you judge all peoples with integrity;
you govern the nations of the earth.

Let the peoples praise you, Lord,
let all the peoples praise you.

The earth gives its harvest.
God, our God, blesses us.
May God bless us indeed
and the ends of the earth revere him.

READING

No matter who you are, you have no excuse for passing judgment on another. When you judge others, you condemn yourself, because you are doing the very same kind of things yourself. We know that God condemns such behavior impartially. Do you think when you judge others who behave like this that you will escape God's judgment? Or are you presuming upon his abundant goodness, patience and forbearance? Do you not know that God's kindness is meant to lead you to repentance?

Romans 2:1-4

CANTICLE

My soul proclaims the greatness of the
 Lord,
my spirit exults in God my Savior;
because he looks upon his lowly handmaid.

Yes, from this day forward
all generations will call me blessed,
for the Almighty does great things for me.

Holy is his name,
his mercy reaches from age to age
for those who fear him.
He shows the power of his arm;
he overthrows the proud of heart,
pulls down the mighty from their thrones,
lifting up the lowly.

The hungry he fills with good things,
the rich he sends away empty.
He comes to the help of Israel his servant,
mindful of his mercy,
remembering the promises made to our
ancestors,
the mercy promised to Abraham
and his descendants for ever.

"Magnificat," Luke 1:46-55

INTERCESSIONS

That God's people may work for the needs and the rights of the poor and powerless: Lord, hear our prayer.

That our nation's leaders may work for the good of all the world: Lord, hear our prayer.

That there be an end to war, poverty and suffering: Lord, hear our prayer.

That those with whom I have worked in the past may be blessed by the promises of the Kingdom: Lord, hear our prayer.

Our Father...

BLESSING

May the grace of our Lord Jesus Christ be with us, and his peace and mercy with all who follow his way. Amen.

Monday
Morning Prayer

CALL TO PRAYER

Let our hearts be ready for the Lord Jesus. Let us welcome him whose glory and power endures for all ages.

HYMN

Father of our Lord Jesus,
as I awaken
to the sounds of your voice
in the morning song of the birds,
to the call of your presence
in the gentle rays of the rising sun,
I pray you will be
my strong right arm
throughout this new day.

You grant life that my living
may be a continual act of praise.
You are the morning light,
showing me the way to be a beacon
of hope for others
who doubt your presence.

Be with me as I go to my daily work.
A new song of praise is in my heart
for you and all you have given to me.

"Morning Prayer" by Basil Arbour
Time Out; Prayers for Busy People

PSALM 18 (19)

The heavens proclaim God's glory,
the skies display the work of his hands.

One day tells the next day,
each night tells the next.
Although we hear no word or sound,
yet their voice reaches the whole world,
their message passes to the ends of the
earth.

He has pitched a tent for the sun.
It emerges like a bridegroom,
rejoices like a champion.

Rising at one end of the heavens,
it runs to the other far side,
nothing escaping its heat.

The Lord's law is perfect,
giving new life to the soul.
The Lord's command is true,
making the simple wise.

The Lord's precepts are righteous,
giving joy to the heart.
The Lord's commands are pure,
giving light to the eye.
The fear of the Lord is holy,
lasting for ever.

The judgments of the Lord are true,
all of them just:
more desirable than gold,

even the finest of gold,
and sweeter than honey,
fresh from the honeycomb.

Thus is your servant taught,
your servant rewarded.
Could I ever know all my own faults?
Cleanse me from my hidden sins.

Preserve your servant from pride,
let it not be my master.
Keep me pure and free from sin.

May the words of my mouth,
the thoughts of my heart,
find favor in your eyes,
Lord, my strength, my Savior.

Psalm 28 (29)

Acknowledge the Lord, children of God,
acknowledge his glory and power.
Acknowledge the glory of his name,
worship the Lord in the glory of his courts.

The voice of the Lord on the waters!
The Lord on the great waters,
the Lord's voice thundering!
The Lord's voice is mighty,
the Lord's voice is glorious!

The voice of the Lord shatters cedars,
the Lord's voice snaps Lebanon's cedars.
He makes Lebanon jump like a calf,
sets Sirion leaping like a wild young bull.

The Lord's voice sharpens lightning's
arrows,
the Lord's voice swirls the desert sands,
whirling the wilderness of Kadesh.

The Lord's voice makes tall terebinth trees
quiver
and strips forests bare.

The God of glory thunders,
in his holy place all things cry "Glory!"
The Lord is enthroned over the flood,
the Lord is enthroned as King for ever.

The Lord gives strength to his people,
the Lord blesses his people with peace.

READING

The Lord said to Abram, "Leave your country, your family and your father's house for the land that I will show you. I will make of you a great nation. I will bless you and make your name so great that it will be used as a blessing. I will bless those who bless you; I will curse those who curse you. All peoples of the earth shall bless themselves by you." So Abram went as the Lord had told him.

Genesis 12:1-4

CANTICLE

Remember the Good News
proclaimed in my preaching:

Jesus Christ, risen from the dead,
is descended from David.

This is a statement we can rely on:
if we have died with him,
we also shall live with him;
if we endure,
we shall also reign with him;
if we deny him, he will deny us —
but though we may be faithless,
he remains faithful.

He cannot deny what is his own self.

2 Timothy 2:8, 11-13

INTERCESSIONS

That the Church truly be a sign pointing to the Kingdom of God in our midst: Lord, show us your light.

That the citizens of our nation be concerned about the people living in the poorer countries of the world: Lord, show us your light.

That those who suffer in mind or body may be convinced of God's love: Lord, show us your light.

That my family, friends and loved ones who have died, and all the faithful departed, may enjoy the peace and mercy of God: Lord, show us your light.

Our Father...

BLESSING

We are called to take our place among the saints. May his Spirit keep us steady and blameless until the day of our Lord Jesus Christ. Amen.

Evening Prayer

CALL TO PRAYER

Holy, holy, holy is the Lord, God the Almighty, who was, and is, and still is to come. With joy let us praise Father, Son and Holy Spirit.

HYMN

We bless you, threefold Light
in one brightness.

You dissolved the dark
and gave us the sun.
You give us the light
of reason and wisdom,
reflecting your heavenly splendor
and the sun's daily glory,
that we might see
light that is not ours
and ourselves become pure light.

You brighten the heavens with the stars.
You order night to follow day in peace.

You give us rest after labor,
but by day you urge us forth to do
what pleases you,
so we learn to shun the dark
and hasten to the day of days
which shall not know night.

Adapted from a hymn
by Saint Gregory of Nazianzus

PSALM 22 (23)

The Lord is my shepherd.
There is nothing that I lack.

Fresh and green are the pastures
in which I lie.
Beside restful waters he leads me
and there refreshes my soul.

He guides me on right paths
for his name's sake.
Though I walk through the valley of dark
shadows
I will fear no evil.

For you are with me.
Your rod and your staff comfort me.

You prepare a table for me
in the sight of my enemies.
You anoint my head with oil,
my cup overflows.

Your goodness and mercy follow me
every day of my life.

I shall live in the house of the Lord
all the days of my life.

PSALM 64 (65)

It is right to praise you, O God, in Zion,
to fulfil the vows made you,
for you answer our prayers.

To you all flesh must come because of sins;
when our misdeeds prevail over us,
you blot them out.

Blessed are those whom you choose,
whom you invite to live in your courts.
We are filled with the good things of your house,
of your holy temple.

You answer us with righteousness,
with awesome deeds, O God, our Savior.
You are the hope of the ends of the earth,
of the distant seas.

By your strength the mountains stand firm,
such is the power which girds you.
You still the roaring of the seas,
the raging of the waves,
and the tumult of the peoples.

Those who dwell at the ends of the earth
are awed by your wonders;

the doors of dawn and dusk proclaim
  your praises.

You tend the earth and give it water,
making it rich and fertile.
The river of God is full,
providing water for the crops.

You drench earth's furrows,
you level its ridges,
you soften it with showers and bless its
  growth.
You crown the year with your bounty;
where you have passed, life's riches
  overflow.

The pastures of the wilderness flow richly,
the hillsides are girded with joy,
the meadows are clothed with sheep,
the valleys are decked in wheat —
they shout and sing for joy!

READING

Whatever you eat, whatever you drink, no matter what you do, do it all for the glory of God. Give offence to nobody — Jews or Greeks or to the Church of God — just as I try to please everyone all the time, not seeking my own advantage but that of everybody else, that they may be saved. Imitate me, as I imitate Christ.

1 Corinthians 10:31 — 11:1

CANTICLE

In victory, sing the song of Moses,
servant of God,
and the song of the Lamb:

Great and wonderful are your deeds,
Lord God Almighty.
Just and true are all your ways,
King of the ages.

Who would not revere and praise
your name, O Lord?
You alone are holy.

All nations shall come and worship you
for the many acts of justice you reveal.

Revelations 15:3-4

INTERCESSIONS

That the Church be always generous to the hungry and the homeless: Lord, your compassion embraces all times and places.

That nations may put their trust in justice and fair dealing and not in bombs and guns: Lord, your compassion embraces all times and places.

That alcoholics and drug addicts may find new strength and hope: Lord, your compassion embraces all times and places.

That my neighborhood may live in peace and joy: Lord, your compassion embraces all times and places.

Our Father...

BLESSING

May the God and Father of our Lord Jesus Christ, our gentle Father who is the God of all consolation, comfort us and all the sorrowing, for he is the God who raises the dead to life. Amen.

Tuesday
Morning Prayer

CALL TO PRAYER

Let our hearts be ready for the Lord Jesus. Let us welcome him whose glory and power endures for all ages.

HYMN

King of kings, Lord of lords,
you alone are immortal.

Living in unapproachable light,
sitting above the heavenly hosts,
riding on the wings of the wind.
You created heavens, lands, seas
and all within them.

The winds are your messengers,
lightning is your servant;
your fingers measure the heavens,
your hand holds the earth.

Everything you made
you have said it is good,
but us you made
in your own image.

Adapted from the ancient prayer,
"A Prayer of Peter and the Other Apostles"

PSALM 56 (57)

Be merciful to me, God, be merciful,
for in you my soul seeks shelter.
In the shadow of your wings I take refuge,
till the destroying storm is over.

I call to God the Most High,
to God who fulfils his purpose for me.
He will send from heaven and save me;
he will send forth his faithfulness and love;
he shames those who trample upon me.

I lie in the midst of lions,
with greedy teeth sharp as spears,
whose tongues are sharpened swords.
Rise up above the heavens, O God,
let your glory be over all the earth.

They set a net for me
as I walk bowed down with care;
they dig a pit for me
but fall in it themselves.

My heart is ready, God, my heart is ready.
I will sing to you and make music.
Awake, my soul; awake, lute and harp;
I will awake the morning.

I will give you thanks, Lord, among the
people,
I will sing your praise among the nations.

The greatness of your mercy reaches to
  the heavens,
your faithfulness to the clouds.

Rise up, O God, above the heavens,
let your glory be over all the earth.

PSALM 23 (24)

The Lord's is the earth
and all that lives on it —
the world and all it holds are his.
He established the world on the oceans,
set it firm amid the seas.

Who shall climb the mountain of the Lord?
Who shall stand in his holy place?

Those who have clean hands and pure
  hearts,
who do not treasure idols
nor make empty promises.

Theirs is the Lord's blessing;
he shall reward them.
Such are they who seek the Lord,
searching for the God of Jacob.

Gates, open up,
doors, open forth,
let the King of glory enter.

Who is the King of glory?
The Lord, mighty and powerful,
the Lord victorious.

Gates, open up,
doors, open forth,
let the King of glory enter.

Who is the King of glory?
The Lord of hosts
is the King of glory.

READING

The angel of the Lord appeared to Moses in a flame of fire in the middle of a bush. He looked and saw that the bush was in flames and yet was not burning. "I must go and see this great sight," Moses said, "and see why the bush is not burnt." When the Lord saw he had come to see, God called to him from the bush, "Moses, Moses." "Here I am," he answered. "Come no nearer. Take off your shoes. The place where you are standing is holy ground. I am the God of your father, the God of Abraham, the God of Isaac, the God of Jacob."

Exodus 3:2-6

CANTICLE

This is the great mystery of our religion:

Manifested in the flesh,
vindicated in the Spirit,
seen by angels,
proclaimed among the nations,
believed in by the world,
taken up in glory.

The appearing of our Lord Jesus Christ
is manifested at the proper moment
by the blessed and only Ruler,
King of kings, Lord of lords,
who alone is immortal,
dwelling in light inaccessible,
whom no human eye has seen or can see:
To him be honor and everlasting power.

1 Timothy 3:16, 6:14-16

INTERCESSIONS

That the people of God may never refuse the gifts of the Spirit: Lord, your love is our life.

That our governments and businesses be mindful of the unemployed and those facing financial ruin: Lord, your love is our life.

That the physically and mentally handicapped be convinced of their dignity and grace: Lord, your love is our life.

That my neighbors who are in distress may gain hope and courage: Lord, your love is our life.

Our Father...

BLESSING

May we be awake to all dangers, firm in the faith, courageous and strong. May we do everything in the love of the Lord. May the God of peace be with us all. Amen.

Evening Prayer

CALL TO PRAYER

Holy, holy, holy is the Lord, God the Almighty, who was, and is, and still is to come. With joy let us praise Father, Son and Holy Spirit.

HYMN

As this day draws to a close
and the last rays of sunlight disappear,
you are on my mind, Lord God.

For this day and its many blessings,
for the good that I have done,
many thanks.

I now close my eyes with confidence,
and with trust in your enduring love for
me.
As I sleep, may your name be praised
by others who now waken
to your morning song.

Even as I sleep to prepare for tomorrow
my prayer is that I may once again
proclaim your goodness and love
in a new day.

"Evening Prayer" by Basil Arbour
Time Out; Prayers for Busy People

PSALM 90 (91)

They who dwell in the shelter of the Most High,
who live under the shadow of the Almighty,
say to the Lord,
"You are my refuge, my stronghold,
my God in whom I trust."

He delivers you from the hunter's snare,
from the destroying plague.
He covers you with his wings;
you are safe under his feathers.
His faithfulness shields and protects you.

Do not fear the terror of the night,
nor arrow that flies by day;
neither the pestilence of the night,
nor the plague that lays waste at noon.

Though a thousand fall at your side,
ten thousand at your right,
it shall not touch you.
You need only look with your own eyes
to see the reward of the ungodly.

The Lord is your refuge;
you have made the Most High your
protection.
No harm shall fall upon you,
no scourge come near your tent.

For he puts his angels in charge of you,
to guard you in all your ways.
They bear you up in their hands,
lest you dash your foot against a stone.
You will tread on lion and adder,
walk over young lion and serpent.

"I deliver them who cling to me.
I will be with them in trouble,
rescuing them and honoring them.
I will give them long, full life,
and show them my salvation."

PSALM 92 (93)

The Lord is King, robed in majesty;
the Lord is clothed in glory,
girded with power.

He established the world,
it cannot be shaken.
Your throne is established from of old;
you are everlasting.

The floods lift up, O Lord,
the floods lift up their voice;
the floods lift up their roaring.

Mightier than the thunders of many waters,
mightier than the sea's roaring waters,
the Lord on high is mighty.

Your decrees are certain;
holiness, Lord, befits your house for ever.

READING

You were called to freedom, my brothers and sisters, but be careful not to use this freedom to indulge yourselves. Instead, serve one another through love, since the whole law is summarized in one word, "Love your neighbor as yourself." But if you snap at one another and tear each other to pieces, be careful that you are not all destroyed. But I say that if you walk by the Spirit, you will not yield to self-indulgence.

Galatians 5:13-16

CANTICLE

The Son is the image of the invisible God,
the first-born of all creation.

For in him were created all things —
in heaven and on earth,
things visible and invisible,
thrones, dominions, sovereignties and
powers —
all things were created through him and
for him.

He is before all things
and all things are united in him.
He is the head of the Church, his body;
he is the beginning, first-born from the
  dead,
that he may be first in every way.

In him the fullness of God is pleased to
  dwell,
to reconcile to himself all things,
everything in heaven and on earth,
making peace by the blood of his cross.

Colossians 1:15-20

INTERCESSIONS

That the Church may reveal to the world the transforming glory of God: Lord, you are our way, our truth and our life.

That our nation foster respect and understanding among all people, no matter what their language, religion or color: Lord, you are our way, our truth and our life.

That the sick and the suffering find health and new life in God's promise: Lord, you are our way, our truth and our life.

That my faith which I have tried to share with my family and friends lead us all to God's everlasting love: Lord, you are our way, our truth and our life.

Our Father...

BLESSING

May God the Father and the Lord Jesus Christ grant peace, love and faith to us and all his people. Amen.

Wednesday Morning Prayer

CALL TO PRAYER

Let our hearts be ready for the Lord Jesus. Let us welcome him whose glory and power endures for all ages.

HYMN

All-holy, from my youth
you have shown me life and light.

All-holy, you are the Father of all.
All-holy, you are before time began.
All-holy, all creatures know you are God.

All-holy, your Word created all things.
All-holy, your light never darkens.
All-holy, you are beyond all praise.

Accept the words of my heart and spirit.
I seek you,
unspeakable One,
beyond all words,
speaking in silence.

Let me not forget who I am:
come to me, strengthen me,
that in your love I may share your grace
with my brothers and sisters,
your sons and daughters.

Adapted from an ancient Christian prayer

PSALM 45 (46)

God is our shelter and strength,
always ready to help in times of trouble.
So we will not fear when the earth quakes,
when mountains topple into the sea.

The Lord of hosts is with us,
the God of Jacob is our refuge.

A river refreshens the city of God,
where the Most High dwells in his holy place.
God is in its midst, it will never fall.
As dawn breaks, God brings his help.
The nations are in uproar, kingdoms are
shaken,
God lifts his voice, the earth trembles.

The Lord of hosts is with us,
the God of Jacob is our refuge.

Come and see the wonders of the Lord,
the astounding things he does on earth.
Over all the world he brings an end to
wars,
breaking bows, snapping spears,
burning chariots with fire.
"Be still. Know that I am God.
I will be acknowledged by the nations,
acclaimed upon earth."

The Lord of hosts is with us,
the God of Jacob is our stronghold.

PSALM 99 (100)

Make a joyful sound to the Lord, all the
earth.
Serve the Lord joyfully,
come into his presence singing.

Know that he, the Lord, is God:
he made us, we belong to him;
we are his people, the sheep of his
pasture.

Come into his gates with thanksgiving,
come into his house with praise.
Give thanks to him, bless his name.

For the Lord is good; his mercy for ever,
his faithfulness continues from age to age.

READING

And Moses said, "Take heed and be on your guard, lest what your eyes have seen you forget and let slip from your heart all the days of your life. Instead, tell it to your children and your children's children. For on the day you stood before the Lord your God at Horeb, the Lord said to me, "Gather the people before me that I may let them hear my words, that they may learn to revere me all the days they live on earth, and may teach this to their children."

Deuteronomy 4:9-10

CANTICLE

In the beginning was the Word:
the Word was with God
and the Word was God.
He was with God in the beginning.

All things were made through him;
nothing is except through him.
In him was life —
that life was the light of humanity,
a light that shone in the dark,
a light darkness could not overpower.

A man came, sent from God,
whose name was John.
He came as a witness,
to bear witness to the light,
that all might believe through him.
He was not the light
but came to bear witness to the light.

The true light that enlightens all people
came into the world.
He was in the world,
but the world did not know him.
He came to his own domain
but his own people did not accept him.

Yet to those who did accept him,
who believed in his name,
he gave power to become
children of God —
born not of blood,

nor of urge of the flesh,
nor of human will,
but of God.

The Word was made flesh.
He dwelt among us,
full of grace and truth.

We saw his glory,
the glory that is his, the Father's only
Son.
From his fullness we all have received,
grace upon grace.

John 1:1-14, 16

INTERCESSIONS

That Christians witness to God's mercy in word and deed: Lord, your glory gives us hope.

That our political and civic leaders be good stewards and servants: Lord, your glory gives us hope.

That the anxious, the fearful and the nervous be made bold by God's Good News: Lord, your glory gives us hope.

That those who have helped and assisted me in any way be rewarded for their kindness and patience: Lord, your glory gives us hope.

Our Father...

BLESSING

May we help one another to grow in unity and peace, living in the presence and fellowship of the God of love and peace. Amen.

Evening Prayer

CALL TO PRAYER

Holy, holy, holy is the Lord, God the Almighty, who was, and is, and still is to come. With joy let us praise Father, Son and Holy Spirit.

HYMN

O Christ, essence of the day,
paring darkness from the night,
you are at the heart of day,
calling us to holy light.

Holy Lord of the night,
we ask you to protect us;
hold us lovingly in embrace,
let peaceful rest refresh us.

Let our hearts converse with you;
with gentle sleep caressing,
enfold us safely in your arms;
your starry shield our blessing.

Adapted from "Christe, qui es et dies,"
a medieval compline hymn

PSALM 120 (121)

I lift up my eyes to the hills;
where shall I find help?
My help comes from the Lord,
who made heaven and earth.

He will not let your foot stumble;
the One who watches over you never
sleeps.
Behold, the guardian of Israel
never slumbers nor sleeps.

The Lord guards you and keeps you,
he is at your right hand —
sun shall not strike you by day
nor the moon by night.

The Lord defends you from all evil;
he guards your life.
The Lord protects your going and coming,
now and for ever.

PSALM 112 (113)

Praise the Lord!
Servants of the Lord, praise the Lord,
praise the name of the Lord.

Blessed be the name of the Lord,
from this time onward and for ever.

From the rising of the sun to its setting,
praised be the name of the Lord.

The Lord is high above the nations,
his glory rises above the heavens.

Who is like the Lord our God,
seated on high
yet caring to look on heaven and earth?

He raises the lowly from the dust,
lifts up the poor from the wastes,
to give them a place among leaders,
among the leaders of his people.

He gives the barren woman a home
and makes her a joyful mother of children.
Praise the Lord!

READING

Out of the riches of his glory, may the Father through his Spirit empower your inner self to grow strong, so that Christ may dwell in your hearts through faith. So that, planted and rooted in love, you will with all the saints have the strength to grasp the breadth and the length and the height and the depth, until knowing the love of Christ which surpasses knowledge, you are filled with all the fullness of God.

Ephesians 3:16-19

CANTICLE

You are worthy to take the scroll
and break open its seals.

You were slain, and with your blood
you bought us for God,
people of every race and language,
from every people and nation,
making us monarchs and priests,
to serve our God
and to reign on earth.

Worthy is the Lamb that was slain
to receive power and riches,
wisdom and might,
honor, glory and blessing.

To the One who sits on the throne,
and to the Lamb,
be blessing and honor,
glory and might for ever and ever.

Revelation 5:9-10, 12, 14

INTERCESSIONS

For all churches, that they may be one as God wills: Lord, hear our prayer.

For those in positions of leadership and responsibility, that they be strong in their service and faithful to their callings: Lord, hear our prayer.

For the victims of economic and political oppression, and for their oppressors, that God may heal them: Lord, hear our prayer.

For those who today join me in listening to and meditating on the word of God, that our hearts be always open: Lord, hear our prayer.

Our Father...

BLESSING

May grace and eternal life be with us and with all who love our Lord. Amen.

Thursday
Morning Prayer

CALL TO PRAYER

Let our hearts be ready for the Lord Jesus. Let us welcome him whose glory and power endures for all ages.

HYMN

Father of Christ, you see all things,
listen to our prayer.
Let us hear the wonderful song
of your Word who knows you
and shares your life.

He lights our way along your paths
for he suffered with us
to protect us.

With your blessing he forsook immortality
to share our life and death,
freeing us from everlasting night.

Adapted from a prayer
by Saint Gregory of Nazianzus

PSALM 94 (95)

Come, let us sing to the Lord,
let us acclaim our rock of safety.

Let us come into his presence with
thanksgiving,
acclaiming him with song.

For the Lord is a great God,
a King greater than all other gods.

In his hand are the depths of the earth;
the peaks of the mountains are his.
The sea belongs to him, he made it;
his hands shaped the land.

Come, let us worship and bow down;
let us kneel before the Lord, our Maker.
For he is our God,
we are his people, the sheep of his
pasture.

O that today you would listen to his voice!
Harden not your hearts as you did at
Meribah,
as on that day at Massah in the wilderness
when your forebears tested me,
put me to the proof,
though they had seen my deeds.

For forty years that generation repelled me,
until I said,
"This is a people whose hearts are in
error,
for they do not know my ways."

I swore in my anger
that not one of them would enter my rest.

PSALM 145 (146)

Praise the Lord!
Praise the Lord, my soul.
I will praise the Lord while I live;
all my life I will praise the Lord.

Do not put your trust in powerful people,
in human beings who cannot save.
They breathe their last
and return to the earth;
that day all their plans perish.

Blessed are they
whose help is the God of Jacob,
whose hope is in the Lord their God.

The God who made heaven and earth,
the sea, and all that these hold.
He keeps faith for ever,
giving justice to those oppressed.

The Lord gives food to the hungry;
he sets captives free.
The Lord gives sight to the blind;
the Lord lifts up those bowed down.

The Lord loves the righteous;
the Lord protects the stranger.
He looks after the widow and orphan,
but the wicked he brings to ruin.

The Lord will reign for ever;
your God, Zion, will always be King.
Praise the Lord!

READING

Thus says the Lord God, the Holy One of Israel: "You shall be saved by returning and resting. In quietness and trust shall be your strength." But you would not. Instead, you said, "We will speed away." Yet the Lord is waiting to be gracious to you. He exalts himself in having mercy on you. For the Lord is a God of justice. Blessed are they who wait for him.

Isaiah 30:15, 18

CANTICLE

That which was from the beginning,
we have heard,
seen with our own eyes,
looked upon,
touched with our own hands:
the Word of life.

Life made manifest —
we saw it,
we proclaim it,
that together we all may have fellowship,
fellowship with the Father
and his Son, Jesus Christ.

May what we are sharing
make our joy complete.

1 John 1:1-4

That God's people be like Mary and treasure God's Word in their hearts: Lord, let your face shine upon us.

That the world be open to the gifts of God: Lord, let your face shine upon us.

That prisoners, victims of injustice, the oppressed and the persecuted find new heart in the Lord: Lord, let your face shine upon us.

That all my loved ones find the peace which surpasses all understanding: Lord, let your face shine upon us.

Our Father...

BLESSING

May our love for one another grow, that we may become pure and blameless, wholly prepared for the day of Christ when we will fully see the glory of God. Amen.

Evening Prayer

CALL TO PRAYER

Holy, holy, holy is the Lord, God the Almighty, who was, and is, and still is to come. With joy let us praise Father, Son and Holy Spirit.

HYMN

I feel like singing —
a song of praise,
of hope, of wonder.

For the gift of life,
and for the ones I love.
For each precious moment
when I can express my love.

For the beauty of creation
which touches me.
For the stillness of each evening,
lighted by the stars of heaven.

For the peacefulness of my heart.
For the promise of tomorrow.
For all of this,
may your name be praised, Lord.

"For Happy Times" by Basil Arbour
Time Out; Prayers for Busy People

PSALM 126 (127)

Unless the Lord builds the house,
those who build it work in vain.
Unless the Lord watches over the city,
those who watch are watching in vain.

It is in vain to rise up early
and go so late to rest,
anxiously eating the bread of toil —
the Lord gives to his beloved in their sleep.

Children are a heritage from the Lord,
the fruit of the womb is his gift.
Like arrows in the hand of a hero
are the children of one's youth.

Happy those who fill their quiver
with this kind of arrow.
They will not be put to shame at the gates
when they dispute with their enemy.

PSALM 113A (114)

When Israel came forth from Egypt,
the people of Jacob from an alien nation,
Judah became his holy place,
Israel his dominion.

The sea looked and fled,
Jordan turned back.
The mountains skipped like rams,
the hills like sheep.

Why was it, sea, that you fled?
What ailed you, Jordan, that you turned
back?
Mountains, why did you skip like rams,
like sheep, you hills?

Tremble, earth, at the presence of the
Lord,
at the presence of the God of Jacob.
He turns rock into a spring of water
and flint into a fountain.

PSALM 133 (134)

Come, bless the Lord,
servants of the Lord,
who stand at night in the house of the
Lord.

Lift up your hands to the holy place
and bless the Lord.

May the Lord bless you from Zion,
the Lord who made heaven and earth.

READING

Be joyful, brothers and sisters, when you have trials, for you know that when your faith is tested it is only to make you steadfast. So let steadfastness have its full effect in you, that you may become perfect, completely developed, lacking in nothing. Happy are those who stand firm when trials come. They who endure will receive the crown of life which God has promised to those who love him.

James 1:2-4. 12

CANTICLE

If I speak with human and angelic tongues
but without love,
I am a noisy gong, a clashing cymbal.

If I have prophetic powers,
understanding all mysteries and knowledge;

if I have the faith to move mountains,
but without love,
then I am nothing.

If I give away all I have,
and deliver my body to be burnt,
but without love,
I gain nothing.

Love is patient and kind.
Love is not jealous or boastful
arrogant or rude.
Love does not rejoice at wrong
but rejoices in right.
Love bears all things,
believes all things,
hopes all things,
endures all things.

Love never ends.
Prophecies will pass away,
tongues will cease,
knowledge will not continue.

For our knowledge is imperfect,
imperfect our prophecy —
when the perfect comes,
the imperfect passes away.
Now we see in a mirror dimly;
then we shall see face to face.

Now I know in part;
then I shall understand fully,
as I will be fully understood.

Meanwhile, these three abide,
faith, hope and love —
but the greatest of these is love.

1 Corinthians 13:1-10, 12-13

INTERCESSIONS

For those called to speak God's word and proclaim the Lord's deeds: Lord, let us share your victory.

For those who protect our nation from crime, disease and injustice: Lord, let us share your victory.

For parents and children, that they may help each other grow through encouragement, respect and love: Lord, let us share your victory.

For the times I have failed in seeing Christ present in my neighbor: Lord, let us share your victory.

Our Father...

BLESSING

May God fulfil all our needs, in Christ Jesus, as only God can. To him be glory for ever and ever. Amen.

Friday
Morning Prayer

CALL TO PRAYER

Let our hearts be ready for the Lord Jesus. Let us welcome him whose glory and power endures for all ages.

HYMN

We thank you for all blessings —
our nature calls you God,
your grace makes you our Father.
We give you the fruit of our lips
and sing to your Son:

Glory to you, Jesus Christ, for your
baptism.
Glory to you for your cross.
Glory to you for your burial.

Glory to you for your rising
and raising us with you.

Glory to your Father,
who has no beginning,
and to your holy, all-holy,
life-giving Spirit,
now and all days.

Adapted from an ancient liturgical
text for the Easter festival

PSALM 41 (42)

As a deer yearns
for running streams,
so my soul yearns
for you, my God.

My soul thirsts for God,
the God of life.
When shall I come
to see his face?

My tears have been my food,
night and day;
all day long people ask,
"Where is your God?"

My soul melts within me.
I remember going to the house of God,
shouting and singing for joy,
the crowd rejoicing.

Why are you so sad, my soul,
why full of sighs?
Put your trust in God.
I will praise him, my Savior, my God.

My soul is heavy
as I remember you
from the land of Jordan
and from the hills of Hermon.

Deep calls to deep
in the roar of your waters.
Your waves and foaming waters
break over me.

Let the Lord show us his mercy in the day.
I will sing his song at night,
praying to the God of my life.

I will say to God my rock,
"Why do you forget me?
Why must I walk in mourning,
oppressed by my enemy?"

With a rending cry to my bones,
my enemies mock me,
all day long asking,
"Where is your God?"

Why are you so sad, my soul,
why so full of sighs?
Put your trust in God;
I will praise him,
my Savior, my God.

PSALM 98 (99)

The Lord is King, let the nations tremble.
He is enthroned on the cherubim; earth
quakes.

The Lord is great in Zion,
he is high above the nations.
Let them praise his great and awesome
name,
for he is the Holy and Mighty One.

You are the Mighty King who loves justice,
you have established righteousness,

you have given justice and fairness to
Jacob.

Acclaim the Lord our God,
bow down before his footstool —
he is holy.

Moses and Aaron were among his priests;
Samuel among those who called on his
name.
They called to the Lord and he answered.
He spoke to them in the pillar of cloud,
they kept his teachings and the law he
gave.

You answered them, Lord our God,
to them you were the God of forgiveness,
although you punish sins.

Acclaim the Lord our God,
bow down before his holy mountain —
the Lord our God is holy.

READING

Come, let us return to the Lord. He has torn us, but he will heal us. He has stricken us, but he will bandage our wounds. After a day or two he will revive us; on the third day he will raise us up that we may live in his presence. Let us know, let us press on to know the Lord. His coming is as sure as the dawn. He will come to us as showers come, like a spring rain watering the earth.

Hosea 6:1-3

CANTICLE

They who have come out of great
tribulation —
who have washed their robes white again
in the blood of the Lamb —
they stand before the throne of God,
serving him night and day in his holy
place.

The One who sits upon the throne
shelters them with his presence.

They shall hunger no more, nor thirst;
sun shall not strike them, nor scorching
heat;
The Lamb at the throne will shepherd
them,
leading them to springs of living water,
and God will wipe away
every tear from their eye.

Revelation 7:14-17

INTERCESSIONS

For those preparing for the sacraments and those who instruct them: Lord, have mercy.

For all nations, that they respond to those hungering for food and thirsting for justice: Lord, have mercy.

For widows and orphans, the bereaved and the sorrowing, that God give them comfort: Lord, have mercy.

For myself and all whom I know, that we be always open to the voice of the Spirit: Lord, have mercy.

Our Father...

BLESSING

May the God of peace make us perfect and holy. May his Spirit keep us safe and blameless in spirit, soul and body, for the coming of our Lord Jesus Christ. Amen.

Evening Prayer

CALL TO PRAYER

Holy, holy, holy is the Lord, God the Almighty, who was, and is, and still is to come. With joy let us praise Father, Son and Holy Spirit.

HYMN

All-wise, all-knowing, all-holy,
our only true King,
maker of the universe,
guardian over all,
guide in the dark and through death,
light on the journey, pilot for the way.

One in voice and mind this evening,
we sing with full hearts and voices:

In your mercy you have called us
(holy is your calling!),
taught us, enlightened us.

We thank you for sharing
your wisdom and life.

Adapted from an ancient Christian prayer

PSALM 62 (63)

O God, you are my God,
my soul thirsts for you,
my flesh longs for you.

As dry, weary land waits for water,
so do I look upon you in the holy place,
awaiting your power and glory.

Your steadfast goodness is better than life.
My lips praise you;
in your name I lift up my hands.

My longing richly satisfied,
I praise you with joyful lips.
I think of you on my bed;
I meditate on you in the night.

For you are my helper;
in the shadow of your wings I sing for joy.
My soul clings to you;
your right hand holds me fast.

Those who seek my life
go down to the depths of the earth.

Delivered to the sword,
they shall be food for jackals.

But the king will rejoice in God;
those who swear by him shall glory,
and the mouths of liars shall be silenced.

PSALM 121 (122)

I rejoiced when they said to me,
"Let us go up to the house of the Lord."
Now our feet are standing
within your gates, Jerusalem.

Jerusalem — a city restored,
where the pilgrims gather in unity.
There the tribes go up, the tribes of the Lord,
as he has commanded,
to give thanks to the name of the Lord.

Here are the seats of judgment,
the thrones of the house of David.

Pray for the peace of Jerusalem:
may those who love you prosper.
Peace be within your walls,
prosperity in your palaces.

For the sake of these, my family and friends,
I pray that peace be with you.
For the sake of the house of the Lord God,
I pray for your happiness.

READING

Clothe yourselves, all of you, with humility toward one another, for "God opposes the proud but favors the humble." So humble yourselves under the mighty hand of God, that at the appointed time he may raise you. Cast all your anxieties on him, for he cares for you. Be calm yet vigilant. Your adversary, the devil, prowls about like a roaring lion, seeking someone to devour. Resist him, firm in faith, knowing your brothers and sisters throughout the world have to suffer the same way. You will have to suffer only a little while, and then the God of all grace, who called you to eternal glory in Christ, will himself restore, strengthen and support you.

1 Peter 5:5-10

CANTICLE

You must be the same in your minds
as Christ Jesus:

Though he was in the form of God,
he did not cling to his equality with God
but emptied himself,
taking the form of a slave.

He became human,
and in human fashion he humbled himself,

becoming obedient to death,
even death on a cross.

But God raised him on high,
bestowing on him the name above every
name —
so that at the name of Jesus all beings,
in heaven, on earth and in the underworld,
should bend their knee,
and every tongue should acclaim,
to the glory of God the Father:

Jesus Christ is Lord!

Philippians 2:5-11

INTERCESSIONS

That Christians be recognized by their love for one another: Lord, make us your new creation.

That politicians, medical personnel, social workers and business people be always respectful of God's little ones: Lord, make us your new creation.

That the homeless and the lost find shelter in God's protection: Lord, make us your new creation.

That instead of condemning others, I learn to forgive as God has forgiven me: Lord, make us your new creation.

Our Father...

BLESSING

May the God of peace, who brought our Lord Jesus Christ back from the dead to become our shepherd, make us ready to do his will in every kind of good action. Amen.

Saturday
Morning Prayer

CALL TO PRAYER

Let our hearts be ready for the Lord Jesus. Let us welcome him whose glory and power endures for all ages.

HYMN

Hail, heavenly Light,
brightest of the messengers
God has sent to us on earth;

You are the fullness of the sun,
more radiant than the stars,
all the tides of time obey your light.

God of God, Only-Begotten,
Son of the Father from all eternity,
without beginning, our heavenly glory!
We your creatures are in need.

Trustingly we pray
that you yourself will come
like the radiant sun
to enlighten us in darkness and gloom,
for we have passed the night
shrouded in the shade of sin and death.

Cynewulf, 9th-century poet

Psalm 26 (27)

The Lord is my light and salvation,
whom shall I fear?
The Lord is my life's stronghold,
what should I be frightened of?

When the wicked come up to me
to devour my flesh,
they stumble and fall.

Even if an army is set against me,
my heart is not frightened.
Though they wage war against me,
my trust remains firm.

One thing I ask of the Lord,
only one thing I need:
to dwell in the Lord's house
all the days of my life,
to enjoy the pleasures of the Lord,
seeking his will in his holy place.

He shelters me,
keeps me safe in his tent,
protects me high on a rock.
He lifts my head above my enemies
who surround me.

I make him offerings of joy.
I sing to him, I make music to the Lord.
Lord, hear my voice when I cry to you,
have mercy on me, answer me.

My heart has told me, "Seek his face."
I am seeking your face, O Lord.
Do not hide your presence from me;
do not turn away from me in anger.

You are my helper.
Do not forsake me, do not leave me,
God of salvation.

Though father and mother forsake me,
the Lord will care for me.

Teach me your ways, O Lord,
lead me on the right path —
because my enemies are waiting.

Do not abandon me to my enemies,
false witnesses who rise against me,
breathing out violence.

I believe I shall see the Lord's goodness
in the land of the living.
Wait for the Lord,
be courageous, be strong;
trust in the Lord.

PSALM 95 (96)

Sing a new song to the Lord;
sing to the Lord, all the earth.

Sing to the Lord, bless his holy name;
proclaim his salvation day after day.
Declare his glory among the nations,
his wonderful deeds among all peoples.

The Lord is great and greatly to be
  praised,
he is to be feared above all gods.
The gods of the nations are idols,
but the Lord made the heavens.

Glory and majesty go before him,
beauty and power are in his holy place.

Give the Lord, you families of nations,
give the Lord glory and power.
Give the Lord the glory of his name;
bring him gifts and come into his courts.

Worship the Lord in the beauty of holiness,
let the whole earth tremble before him.
Say among the nations, "The Lord is King.
He made the world firm, it shall not be
  moved.
He will judge all peoples with fairness."

Let the heavens be glad, the earth rejoice;
let the sea roar and everything in it.
Let the fields rejoice and all that is in
  them;
let the trees in the woods be glad,
crying out with joy to the Lord.

For he comes, he comes to judge the
  earth.
He shall judge the earth with
  righteousness,
and the peoples with his truth.

READING

Proclaim that the Lord has saved his people, the remnant of Israel. Behold, I bring them back from the land of the north and gather them from the ends of the earth. All of them: the blind and the lame, women with child, women in labor. It is a great company that returns here. They had left in tears, but as I lead them back I console them. I will guide them to streams of water, along a straight path on which they shall not stumble. For I am a father to Israel, and Ephraim is my first-born.

Jeremiah 31:7-9

CANTICLE

Blessed be the God and Father
of our Lord Jesus Christ.
He blesses us in Christ
with every spiritual blessing from heaven.

Even before the world was made,
he chose us, chose us in Christ,
to be holy and blameless before him.

He destined us in love
to be his children through Jesus Christ,
according to his saving will,
that we may praise his glorious grace
which he gives freely to us in his Beloved.

We are redeemed in him through his
blood,

our sins are forgiven,
the riches of his grace lavished upon us.

He has made known to us,
in all wisdom and insight,
the mystery of his will,
his saving plan in Christ,
which had been hidden from the beginning:
that in the fullness of time,
all things would be united in him,
everything in heaven and everything on
earth.

In him, we have been chosen and destined
to live for the praise of God's glory.

Ephesians 1:3-12

INTERCESSIONS

For the Pope, the bishops, priests, ministers, religious and all God's faithful people, that they be enheartened by God's grace: Lord, guide us in your love.

For those who labor, that their work and hope bear good fruit: Lord, guide us in your love.

For families that are separated and friends who are estranged, that they be guided by God's providence: Lord, guide us in your love.

For those who share and bear with me, that God reward them for their patience and concern: Lord, guide us in your love.

Our Father...

BLESSING

May we grow in the grace and knowledge of our Lord and Savior, Jesus Christ, to whom be glory, now and for eternity. Amen.

Evening Prayer

CALL TO PRAYER

Holy, holy, holy is the Lord, God the Almighty, who was, and is, and still is to come. With joy let us praise Father, Son and Holy Spirit.

HYMN

My lamp alight in my hand,
Bridegroom, I come to meet you.

The cry comes from the heights,
awakening the dead:
"Go forth to meet the Bridegroom,
take your lamp, dress in your best.
Wake up, go forth, meet your King."

Joy to you, Christ, Lord of life's dance,
Light of my days, undimmed by the
evening.

With joy and praise
I bring my gifts to you —
Flower of all blossoms, my Love and my Joy,
Wisdom to my mind, the Word for my heart.

Standing at your door,
we welcome your guests.
Dressed like you in wedding clothes,
we celebrate your marriage feast and ours,
for we are your virgin bride.

My lamp alight in my hand,
Bridegroom, I come to meet you.

Adapted from Origen's
"The Virgins' Hymn to Christ"

PSALM 44 (45)

My heart overflows with a noble theme:
I address my poem to the king,
my tongue ready like the pen of a scribe.

You are the fairest of humanity's children;
grace flows from your lips,
for God has blessed you for ever.

Gird your sword at your thigh,
O mighty one, in glory and majesty.
Ride forth in splendor and glory,
in the cause of justice and truth.

Your right hand teaches an awesome lesson,

your arrows sharp, nations are at your
mercy.
Your throne is the throne of God;
your royal scepter the scepter of
righteousness;
you love justice and hate evil.

Therefore God, your God, has anointed you
with the oil of gladness, above your
fellows.
Your robes are fragrant with aloes and
myrrh,
music from ivory palaces gladdens your
heart.
Daughters of kings are among your noble
women.
At your right stands the queen,
in gold from Ophir.

Listen, my daughter, turn your ear.
Forget your own people and your parents'
home.
The king desires your beauty.
He is your lord, bow before him.

O daughter of Tyre,
the wealthiest nations will bring you gifts.

The daughter of the king is glorious,
dressed in robes woven with gold.
Dressed in robes of many colors,
she is led before you, O king,

with her companions.
They enter the palace of the king,
with joy and gladness.

In place of ancestors, you shall have
children;
you will make them rulers over all the
earth.
I shall make your name remembered for
ages,
nations will sing your praise for ever.

PSALM 148

Praise the Lord!
Praise the Lord from the heavens,
praise him in the heights.

Praise him, all his angels,
praise him, heavenly hosts.

Praise him, sun and moon;
praise him, shining stars.

Praise him, highest heavens
and waters above the heavens.

Let them praise the name of the Lord,
for he commanded and they were made.
He established them for ever,
his law shall not pass away.

Praise the Lord from the earth;
praise him, sea monsters and the deeps;
fire and hail, snow and mist,
storms that obey his command;

Mountains and hills,
fruit trees and forests,
wild beasts and tame,
creeping things and flying birds;

Monarchs of the earth, and all peoples,
rulers and leaders of the world,
youths and maidens,
elderly and children;

Let them praise the name of the Lord,
for his name alone is exalted.
His glory is above heaven and earth.
He raises a horn of fortune for his people.

He is the praise of all his servants,
the children of Israel,
the people who are near him.
Praise the Lord!

READING

Christ is all and in all. So, as God's chosen ones, beloved and holy, put on compassion, kindness, humility, gentleness and patience. Bear with one another. Forgive each other as soon as there is something to complain about. As the Lord has forgiven you, so must you forgive. Above all, put on love, which unites everything together in perfect harmony. And let the peace of Christ reign in your hearts, for indeed you have been called to be in one body. Always be thankful. Let the word of Christ live in you in all its richness.

Colossians 3:11-16

CANTICLE

I saw a new heaven and a new earth.
The first heaven and earth had passed away,
and there was no longer any sea.
I saw a holy city,
the new Jerusalem,
coming down out of heaven from God,
as beautiful as a bride dressed for her husband.

I heard a great voice say from the throne:
"Behold the city where God dwells with humanity.
He dwells among them;
they are his people, he is their God.
God himself is with them,
wiping every tear from their eyes.
Death shall be no more,
neither pain, nor mourning, nor sadness.
The world of the past is gone."

He who sits on the throne announces,
"Behold, I make all things new."

Revelation 21:1-5

INTERCESSIONS

For all who believe in God, that their gifts of faith and love lead our world to new hope: Lord, strengthen us.

For all citizens of this land, that they be responsive to their freedom and duty: Lord, strengthen us.

For those suffering from incurable disease, for the lonely, the embittered and the depressed, that they not lose heart: Lord, strengthen us.

For all today listening to God's word, that we like Mary may respond generously: Lord, strengthen us.

Our Father...

BLESSING

May the God of all grace who calls us to eternal glory in Christ see that all is well with us. May his Spirit confirm, strengthen and support us. Amen.

3

Milestones of Faith and Moments for Prayer

Daily Favorites

LORD'S PRAYER

Our Father, who art in heaven,
hallowed by thy name;
thy Kingdom come,
thy will be done on earth
as it is in heaven.
Give us this day our daily bread;
and forgive us our trespasses
as we forgive those who trespass against
us.
And lead us not into temptation,
but deliver us from evil.

DOXOLOGY

For thine is the Kingdom,
the power and the glory,
for ever and ever.

GLORY BE

Glory be to the Father,
and to the Son,
and to the Holy Spirit.
As it was in the beginning,
is now,
and ever shall be,
world without end.

THRICE HOLY

Holy is God!
Holy and strong One,
holy immortal One,
have mercy on us.

HAIL MARY

Hail, Mary, full of grace,
the Lord is with thee.
Blessed art thou among women,
and blessed is the fruit
of thy womb, Jesus.
Holy Mary, Mother of God,
pray for us sinners, now
and at the hour of our death.

Grace before Meals

(1)

Bless us, O Lord,
and these thy gifts
which we are about to receive
from thy bounty,
through Christ our Lord.

(2)

The eyes of all look to you, O Lord,
to give them their food in due season.
You open wide your hands

and fill all things with your blessings,
through Christ our Lord.

Grace after Meals

(1)

We give thee thanks,
Almighty God,
for all thy gifts
which we have received,
through Christ our Lord.

(2)

For these and his many mercies,
may the Lord's name be blessed,
now and for ever,
through Christ our Lord.

MORNING OFFERING

(1)

O Jesus,
through the Immaculate Heart of Mary,
I offer thee my prayers, works,
joys and sufferings of this day,
in union with the holy sacrifice
of the Mass throughout the world.
I offer them
for all the intentions of thy Sacred Heart:
the salvation of souls,

reparation for sins,
the unity of all Christians.
I offer them
for the intentions of our bishops
and in particular for those recommended
by our Holy Father the Pope for this
month.

(2)

Almighty Father, we thank you
for the light and life of a new day.
Keep us safe today
and protect us from every evil.
We offer ourselves this day to you
through Jesus Christ your Son.
May your Holy Spirit
make our thoughts, words and actions
pleasing in your sight.

ACT OF CONTRITION

(1)

O my God, I am heartily sorry
for having offended thee,
and I detest all my sins
because of thy just punishments
but most of all because they offend thee,
my God, who art all good
and deserving of all my love.
I firmly resolve
with the help of thy grace

to confess my sins,
to do penance and to amend my life.

(2)

Have mercy on us, Father,
for love of our Lord Jesus Christ,
who died and rose to save us.

CONFITEOR

I confess to Almighty God,
to blessed Mary ever Virgin,
to blessed Michael the Archangel,
to blessed John the Baptist,
to the holy apostles Peter and Paul,
and to all the saints,
that I have sinned exceedingly
in thought, word and deed,
through my fault,
through my fault,
through my most grievous fault.
Therefore I beseech
blessed Mary ever Virgin,
blessed Michael the Archangel,
blessed John the Baptist,
the holy apostles Peter and Paul,
and all the saints,
to pray to the Lord our God for me.

ACT OF FAITH

(1)

Lord, I believe.
Help my unbelief.

(2)

O my God, I firmly believe
that you are one God
in three divine persons,
Father, Son and Holy Spirit;
I believe that your divine Son became man
and died for our sins,
and that he will come to judge
the living and the dead.
I believe these and all the truths
which the holy Catholic Church teaches,
because you have revealed them
who can neither deceive nor be deceived.

ACT OF HOPE

(1)

O my God, relying
on your infinite goodness and promises,
I hope to obtain pardon for my sins,
the help of your grace,
and life everlasting,
through the merits of Jesus Christ,
my Lord and Redeemer.

(2)

O God, you have given us Jesus
to be our supreme high priest.
Help us never to let go of the faith
which he has given us.
We hope in him
because he felt our weaknesses with us
and was tempted in every way that we are,
although he was without sin.
Give us his Spirit of trust
that we may approach your throne of
grace,
confident in your mercy.

ACT OF LOVE

(1)

O my God, I love you above all things,
with my whole heart and soul,
because you are all good
and worthy of all love.
I love my neighbor as myself
for love of you.
I forgive all who have injured me
and I ask pardon of all
whom I have injured.

(2)

O God, we believe that you are love
and that you love us.
Help us to live in love

that we may live in you and you in us.
Send us your Spirit of love
that we may love as Jesus loved,
for he has taught us
that we cannot love you
if we do not love one another.

APOSTLES' CREED

I believe in God, the Father Almighty,
Creator of heaven and earth.

I believe in Jesus Christ,
his only Son, our Lord,
who was conceived of the Holy Spirit,
born of the Virgin Mary,
suffered under Pontius Pilate,
was crucified, died and was buried;
he descended into hell;
the third day he arose again from the dead;
he ascended into heaven and sits
at the right hand of God, the Father Almighty;
he shall come again
to judge the living and the dead.

I believe in the Holy Spirit,
the holy Catholic Church,
the communion of saints,
the forgiveness of sins,
the resurrection of the body,
and life everlasting.

DIVINE PRAISES

Blessed be God.
Blessed be his holy name.
Blessed be Jesus Christ, true God and true man.
Blessed be the name of Jesus.
Blessed be his most sacred Heart.
Blessed be his most precious blood.
Blessed be Jesus in the most holy sacrament of the altar.
Blessed be the Holy Spirit, the Paraclete.
Blessed be the great Mother of God, Mary most holy.
Blessed be her holy and immaculate conception.
Blessed be her glorious assumption.
Blessed be the name of Mary, virgin and mother.
Blessed be Saint Joseph, her most chaste spouse.
Blessed be God in his angels and in his saints.

TE DEUM

We praise you, O God.
We acclaim you as Lord.
Eternal Father, all the earth worships you.
All the angels, the heavens, the heavenly hosts,

the cherubim and seraphim,
in one unending song
proclaim:

Holy, holy, holy Lord, God of power and might,
heaven and earth are full of your glory.

The glorious band of apostles praises you.
The many prophets glorify you.
Your white-robed martyrs sing your glory.
Throughout all the earth,
your holy Church acclaims you:

Father of boundless majesty,
your truly Only Begotten
who is worthy of our worship,
and your Holy Spirit, our friend and guide.

You are the King of glory, O Christ,
eternal Son of the Father.
When you became man so as to set us free
you did not disdain the Virgin's womb.
You overcame the pangs of death,
opening for all believers
the Kingdom of heaven.
You are seated at God's right hand,
in the Father's glory.
We believe you will come to be our judge.
Lord, come, help your family,
redeemed by your blood.

Bring us with your saints
to your unending glory.

Save your people, Lord,
and bless your inheritance;
guide and uphold us for ever.

Day by day we bless you;
we praise your name always.

Keep us this day free from all sin;
have mercy on us, Lord, have mercy.

Show us your loving kindness;
for we put all our trust in you.

In you, Lord, is our hope.
Do not let us come to nothing.

HYMN OF THE THREE YOUNG MEN

Blessed are you, Lord, God of our
ancestors,
may you be praised and glorified for ever.
Blessed is your holy name,
praised and glorified for ever.
Blessed is your holy temple,
praised and glorified for ever.
Blessed is the throne of your Kingdom,
praised and glorified for ever.
Blessed are you in the depths
and enthroned in the heights,
praised and glorified for ever.
Blessed are you in the heaven of heavens,
praised and glorified for ever.

Bless the Lord, all things the Lord has
made,
praise and acclaim him for ever.

Bless the Lord, you the Lord's angels.
Bless the Lord, you heavens.
Bless the Lord, waters above the heavens.
Bless the Lord, you heavenly hosts.
Bless the Lord, sun and moon.
Bless the Lord, each drop of rain and dew.
Bless the Lord, all you winds.
Bless the Lord, fire and heat.
Bless the Lord, cold and winter.
Bless the Lord, frost and cold.
Bless the Lord, snow and ice.
Bless the Lord, day and night.
Bless the Lord, light and dark.
Bless the Lord, lightning and storm.

Let the earth too bless the Lord.
Praise and acclaim him for ever.
Bless the Lord, mountains and hills.
Bless the Lord, all growing things.
Bless the Lord, springs of water.
Bless the Lord, seas and rivers.
Bless the Lord, sea creatures
and everything that lives in the waters.
Bless the Lord, all you birds
that fly in the skies.
Bless the Lord, animals wild and tame.

Bless the Lord, sons and daughters of
the human race.

Let Israel bless the Lord,
praise and acclaim him for ever.
Bless the Lord, priests of the Lord.
Bless the Lord, servants of the Lord.
Bless the Lord, spirits of the faithful.
Bless the Lord, all dedicated and humble
hearts.

Ananias, Azarias and Mizael, bless the
Lord,
praise and acclaim him for ever.
He has snatched us from the realm of
death,
saved us from destruction,
rescued us from the fiery furnace,
delivered us from the flames.

Give thanks to the Lord; he is good
and his love is everlasting.
All you who worship him,
bless God the Most High,
praise him and thank him,
for everlasting is his love.

Daniel 3:52-90

Prayers to Our Lord Jesus Christ

APOSTLES' CONFESSION

Lord, we believe.
You have the message of eternal life.
You are the Holy One of God.

John 6:68

JESUS PRAYER

Lord Jesus,
have mercy on me, a sinner.

The Jesus Prayer, a favorite especially in the Eastern Churches of the Slavic tradition, is repeated as a litany until it becomes part of one's heart.

ANIMA CHRISTI

Soul of Christ, make me holy.
Body of Christ, save me.
Blood of Christ, inebriate me.
Water from the side of Christ, wash me clean.
Passion of Christ, strengthen me.
Kind Jesus, hear me.
Hide me within your wounds.
Let me never be separated from you.
Defend me from evil.
In the hour of my death
call me to yourself,
that with your saints I may praise you
in everlasting life. Amen.

PRAYER BEFORE A CRUCIFIX

Good and dearest Jesus,
I kneel before thee,
beseeching and praying thee
with all my heart and soul
to engrave deep and living signs
of faith, hope and love upon my heart,
with true repentance for my sins
and a firm resolve to make amends.
I ponder thy five wounds,
dwelling upon them with compassion,
and recall the words
the prophet David spoke long ago about thee:
they have pierced my hands and feet;
they have numbered all my bones.

CONSECRATION TO THE SACRED HEART

Most kind Jesus, Redeemer of the human race,
look down upon us
humbly prostrate before thine altar.
We are thine and thine we wish to be,
but to be more surely united to thee,
behold we individually today
freely consecrate ourselves
to thy most sacred Heart.

Many indeed have never known thee.
Many too, despising thy commands,

have rejected thee.
Have mercy on us all,
most merciful Jesus,
and draw all people to thy sacred Heart.

Be King, Lord, not only of the faithful
who have never forsaken thee,
but also of thy prodigal children
who have abandoned thee,
and lead them quickly to their Father's
house,
lest they perish of misery and hunger.

Be King over those misled by error
and call them to the harbor of truth
and the unity of faith,
so that soon there may be one fold
and one Shepherd.

Be King over all unbelievers.
Deliver them out of darkness into light
and into the Kingdom of God.
Grant, O Lord, safety to thy Church.
Give peace and order to all nations.
Make the earth resound from pole to pole
with one cry:
Praise to the divine Heart
that wrought our salvation.
To it be glory and honor for ever.

LITANY OF THE HOLY NAME OF JESUS

Lord, have mercy on us.
Christ, have mercy on us.
Lord, have mercy on us.
Jesus, hear us.
Jesus, graciously hear us.

God the Father of heaven, *have mercy on us.*
God the Son, Redeemer of the world,...
God the Holy Spirit,...
Holy Trinity, one God,...
Jesus, Son of the living God,...
Jesus, splendor of the Father,...
Jesus, brightness of eternal light,...
Jesus, King of glory,...
Jesus, sun of justice,...
Jesus, son of the Virgin Mary,...
Jesus, most amiable,...
Jesus, most admirable,...
Jesus, mighty God,...
Jesus, father of the world to come,...
Jesus, angel of great counsel,...
Jesus, most powerful,...
Jesus, most patient,...
Jesus, most obedient,...
Jesus, meek and humble of heart,...
Jesus, lover of chastity,...
Jesus, lover of us,...
Jesus, God of peace,...

Jesus, author of life,...
Jesus, model of virtues,...
Jesus, zealous for souls,...
Jesus, our God,...
Jesus, our refuge,...
Jesus, father of the poor,...
Jesus, treasure of the faithful,...
Jesus, good shepherd,...
Jesus, true light,...
Jesus, eternal wisdom,...
Jesus, infinite goodness,...
Jesus, our way and our life,...
Jesus, joy of angels,...
Jesus, King of patriarchs,...
Jesus, master of apostles,...
Jesus, teacher of evangelists,...
Jesus, strength of martyrs,...
Jesus, light of confessors,...
Jesus, purity of virgins,...
Jesus, crown of all saints,...

Be merciful; spare us, O Jesus.
Be merciful; graciously hear us, O Jesus.
From all evil, *Jesus, deliver us.*
From all sin,...
From your wrath,...
From the snares of the devil,...
From the spirit of immorality,...
From everlasting death,...
From neglecting your inspiration,...
Through the mystery of your holy
incarnation,...

Through your nativity,...
Through your infancy,...
Through your most divine life,...
Through your labors,...
Through your agony and passion,...
Through your cross and abandonment,...
Through your sufferings,...
Through your death and burial,...
Through your resurrection,...
Through your ascension,...
Through your institution of the holy Eucharist,...
Through your joys,...
Through your glory,...

Lamb of God, you take away the sins of the world, spare us, O Lord.
Lamb of God, you take away the sins of the world, graciously hear us, O Lord.
Lamb of God, you take away the sins of the world, have mercy on us.
Jesus, hear us.
Jesus, graciously hear us.

Lord Jesus Christ, you said:
Ask and you shall receive,
seek and you shall find,
knock and it shall be opened to you;
we ask you to give us the gift
of always loving you with all our hearts,
and of never ceasing to praise you
in all our words and deeds.

LITANY OF THE SACRED HEART

Lord, have mercy on us.
Christ, have mercy on us.
Lord, have mercy on us.
Christ, hear us.
Christ, graciously hear us.
God the Father of heaven, have mercy on us.
God the Son, Redeemer of the world, have mercy on us.
God the Holy Spirit, have mercy on us.
Holy Trinity, one God, have mercy on us.
Heart of Jesus, Son of the Eternal Father, *have mercy on us.*
Heart of Jesus, formed by the Holy Spirit in the womb of the Virgin Mother,...
Heart of Jesus, substantially united to the Word of God,...
Heart of Jesus, of infinite majesty,...
Heart of Jesus, sacred temple of God,...
Heart of Jesus, tabernacle of the Most High,...
Heart of Jesus, house of God and gate of heaven,...
Heart of Jesus, burning furnace of charity,...
Heart of Jesus, abode of justice and love,...
Heart of Jesus, full of goodness and love,...
Heart of Jesus, abyss of all virtues,...
Heart of Jesus, worthy of all praise,...

Heart of Jesus, King and center of all hearts,...
Heart of Jesus, in whom are all the treasures of wisdom and knowledge,...
Heart of Jesus, in whom dwells the fullness of divinity,...
Heart of Jesus, in whom the Father was well pleased,...
Heart of Jesus, of whose fullness we have all received,...
Heart of Jesus, desire of the everlasting hills,...
Heart of Jesus, patient and most merciful,...
Heart of Jesus, enriching all those who invoke you,...
Heart of Jesus, fountain of life and holiness,...
Heart of Jesus, propitiation for our sins,...
Heart of Jesus, loaded down with reproach,...
Heart of Jesus, bruised for our offences,...
Heart of Jesus, obedient unto death,...
Heart of Jesus, pierced with a lance,...
Heart of Jesus, source of all consolation,...
Heart of Jesus, our life and resurrection,...
Heart of Jesus, our peace and reconciliation,...
Heart of Jesus, victim for sin,...
Heart of Jesus, salvation for those who trust in you,...

Heart of Jesus, hope of those who die in you,...
Heart of Jesus, delight of all the saints,...

Lamb of God, you take away the sins of the world, spare us, O Lord.
Lamb of God, you take away the sins of the world, graciously hear us, O Lord.
Lamb of God, you take away the sins of the world, have mercy on us.

Jesus, meek and humble of heart,
make our hearts like unto yours.

Almighty and eternal God,
look upon the heart of your beloved Son
and upon the praise and satisfaction
he offers you in the name of sinners
and for those who seek your mercy;
grant us your pardon
in the name of your Son, our Lord, Jesus Christ.

WAY OF THE CROSS

First station.
Jesus is condemned to death.

We adore you, O Christ,
and we praise you,
because by your holy cross
you have redeemed the world.

Jesus, scourged and crowned with thorns, was unjustly condemned to die on the cross. But he accepted this condemnation in order to save us and all the world from sin and death.

Sing, my tongue, the glorious battle,
sing that last and dread affray;
o'er the cross, the Victor's trophy!
Sound the high triumphal lay,
how the pains of death enduring,
earth's Redeemer won the day.

Second station.
Jesus takes up his cross.

We adore you, O Christ,
and we praise you,
because by your holy cross
you have redeemed the world.

Jesus made the journey of his death and passion with humble, self-giving love. His patience and resignation encourage us to take up our cross in the same spirit.

He our Maker, deeply grieving
that the first-made Adam fell
when he ate the fruit forbidden,
whose reward was death and hell,
even then this tree electing,
the first tree's ruin to dispel.

Third station.
Jesus falls the first time.

We adore you, O Christ,
and we praise you,
because by your holy cross
you have redeemed the world.

It is said that Jesus stumbled under the weight of the cross and the sins of the world. Yet he continued on, encouraging us to rise up when we falter and fail.

Thus the work of our salvation
was of old in order laid,
that the manifold deceiver's
art by art would be outweighed;
so the lure the foe put forward
was into means of healing made.

**Fourth station.
Jesus meets his mother.**

We adore you, O Christ,
and we praise you,
because by your holy cross
you have redeemed the world.

The Son of God met the mother of all humanity on the way of the cross. Sharing their compassion, we are to see the Lord present in all who suffer — for they are God's chosen.

Therefore, when eventually the fullness
of the appointed time had come,
he was sent, the world's Creator;
from the Father's heavenly home.
He came forth, in human fashion,
offspring of the Virgin's womb.

Fifth station.
Jesus is helped by Simon of Cyrene.

We adore you, O Christ,
and we praise you,
because by your holy cross
you have redeemed the world.

Even in the midst of the worst suffering and cruelty the Spirit of love is at work. May we be always prompted by that Spirit to assist those around us in need — for what we do to another, we do to the Lord.

God-made-man an infant crying
in a barn where oxen stand,
while the mother-maid his members
wraps in lowly swaddling bands —
tattered rags in comfort winding
round God's human feet and hands.

Sixth station.
Veronica wipes Jesus' face with her veil.

We adore you, O Christ,
and we praise you,
because by your holy cross
you have redeemed the world.

Veronica wiped the face of Jesus with her veil — and found there the miraculous likeness of the Lord. By responding to Jesus present in our midst, we ourselves take on God's likeness.

Thirty years among us dwelling,
his appointed time fulfilled;
born for this, he meets his passion,
freely making his own God's will.
On the cross the Lamb is lifted,
there his blood for all he spills.

Seventh station.
Jesus falls the second time.

We adore you, O Christ,
and we praise you,
because by your holy cross
you have redeemed the world.

Although Jesus was overwhelmed by the weight of the cross, yet he continued on his way. We too are called to persevere on our journey of faith, no matter how futile our efforts seem, because our journey is his.

He endured the nails, the spitting,
vinegar, and spear, and reed.
From his holy body broken,
blood and water forth proceed;
earth and stars, the sky and ocean
by that flood from stain are freed.

Eighth station.
Jesus speaks to the women of Jerusalem.

We adore you, O Christ,
and we praise you,
because by your holy cross
you have redeemed the world.

The women of Jerusalem wept for Jesus but he said to them, “Weep not for me but for yourselves and your children.” The cross of Christ always calls us to repentance — to change our hearts every day of our lives.

Faithful cross, above all others,
one and only noble tree;
none in foliage, none in blossom,
none in fruit thy peer may be.
Sweetest wood and kindest iron,
our dearest weight hangs on thee.

Wipo, 11th century

Ninth station.
Jesus falls a third time.

We adore you, O Christ,
and we praise you,
because by your holy cross
you have redeemed the world.

Even though Jesus may have fallen — for he was like us in all things but sin — he found the strength and courage to continue on. He gives us the same strength and courage, no matter how helpless we feel, to share with him in the world's redemption.

Bend thy boughs, O tree of glory,
thy relaxing sinews bend;
for a while thy ancient rigor
thou wast born with, now suspend,
and the King of heavenly beauty
on thy bosom gently tend.

Tenth station.
Jesus is stripped of his garments.

We adore you, O Christ,
and we praise you,
because by your holy cross
you have redeemed the world.

The executioners stripped Jesus and took his clothes, gambling over who would keep them. We also must be ready to be stripped of all we have and own, that God may truly make us his.

Thou alone was counted worthy
this world's ransom to uphold;
for a shipwrecked race preparing
harbor, as did Noah's ark of old,
but with sacred blood anointed
that from the Paschal Lamb did fall.

Eleventh station.
Jesus is nailed to the cross.

We adore you, O Christ,
and we praise you,
because by your holy cross
you have redeemed the world.

As they crucified Jesus, he prayed, "Father, forgive them — they know not what they do." Crucified with Jesus, we are called by his Spirit to bring forgiveness and reconciliation to all the world.

To the Trinity be glory,
now and always, as is meet;
equal to the Father's honor
is the Son's and Paraclete's;
Threefold One, eternal praises
all created things repeat.

"Pange Lingua,"
Venantius Fortunatus, 530-609

Twelfth station.
Jesus dies on the cross.

We adore you, O Christ,
and we praise you,
because by your holy cross
you have redeemed the world.

Jesus breathed forth his spirit, praying, "Into your hands, Father, I commit my spirit." Through Christ's suffering and death, God brought healing and unity to the world. To share in the Father's healing love, we surrender our life and death into his hands.

The holy paschal work is wrought,
the victim's praise be told.
The loving Shepherd has brought
the sheep into his fold.
The Just and Innocent was slain
to reconcile us to God again.

Thirteenth station.
Jesus is taken down from the cross.

We adore you, O Christ,
and we praise you,
because by your holy cross
you have redeemed the world.

It was accomplished. Joseph of Arimathea took Jesus' body down from the cross, while the women who followed Jesus watched and waited. We too must trust, waiting in vigilance and patience, for God to work his wonderful deeds even in our suffering and death.

Death from the Lord of life has fled,
the awesome fight is over;
behold, he lives now who was dead,
lives on now and for ever.
Mary, you sought him on that day,
tell what you saw on the way.

Fourteenth station.
Jesus is laid in the tomb.

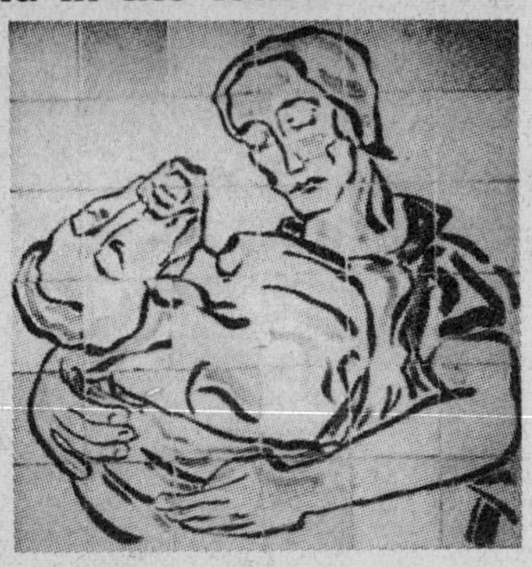

We adore you, O Christ,
and we praise you,
because by your holy cross
you have redeemed the world.

The body of Jesus is wrapped in a shroud and laid in a tomb hewn out of rock. It was sealed with a stone, and the women prepared spices with which to anoint his body. But God brought forth life from death, light from darkness — the same life and light he brings forth in us.

"I saw the empty cavern's gloom,
the garments of the prison,
the angels guarding Jesus' tomb
and the glory of the Risen."
We know Christ rose from the grave
as Victor King the world to save.

"Victimae Paschali,"
Wipo, 11th century

Prayers to the Holy Spirit

COME, HOLY SPIRIT

Come, Holy Spirit,
fill the hearts of the faithful.
Enkindle in them the fire of your love.

Send forth your Spirit
and they shall be created;
and you shall renew
the face of the earth.

VENI SANCTE SPIRITUS

Holy Spirit! Lord of light!
From thy clear celestial height,
thy pure beaming radiance give.

Come, thou father of the poor!
Come with treasures which endure;
come, thou light of all that live!

Thou, of all consolers best,
visiting the troubled breast,
dost refreshing peace bestow;

Thou in toil art comfort sweet;
pleasant coolness in the heat;
solace in the midst of woe.

Light immortal! Light divine!
visit thou these hearts of thine,
and our inmost being fill.

If thou take thy grace away,
nothing pure in us will stay;
all our good is turned away.

Bend the stubborn heart and will;
melt the frozen, warm the chill;
guide the steps that go astray.

Thou, on us who evermore
thee confess and thee adore,
in thy sevenfold gifts descend.

Give us comfort when we die;
give us life with thee on high;
give us joys which never end.

Sequence for Pentecost
Stephen Langton, died 1223

SEVEN GIFTS OF THE HOLY SPIRIT

Knowledge: knowing the Father and Jesus whom he sent;

Wisdom: seeing things as God sees them;

Understanding: grasping God's revelation;

Counsel: knowing what to do in difficulties;

Fortitude: courageously doing what must be done;

Piety: loving God as our Father and Mother, and seeing Jesus in all people;

Fear of the Lord: having reverence and awe for God's word and deed.

Based on Isaiah 11:1-2

TWELVE FRUITS OF THE HOLY SPIRIT

This is what the Spirit brings: love, joy, peace, patience, kindness, goodness, long-suffering, gentleness, faith, modesty, self-control, chastity.

Based on Galatians 5:22

Devotions to the Blessed Virgin Mary

ANGELUS

The angel of the Lord declared unto Mary,
and she conceived of the Holy Spirit.

Hail Mary...

Behold, the handmaid of the Lord;
be it done to me according to thy word.

Hail Mary...

And the word was made flesh;
and dwelt among us.

Hail Mary...

Pray for us, O holy Mother of God;
that we may be made worthy
of the promises of Christ.

Pour forth, we beseech thee, O Lord,
thy grace into our hearts,
that we to whom the message of thy Son
was made known by an angel,
may by his passion and death
be brought to the glory of his resurrection,
through the same Christ our Lord.

REGINA COELI

O Queen of heaven, rejoice, alleluia!
For he whom thou didst deserve to bear,
alleluia!

is risen as he said. Alleluia!
Pray for us to God, alleluia!

Rejoice and be glad,
O Virgin Mary, alleluia!
For the Lord is truly risen, alleluia!

O God,
by the resurrection of thy Son, our Lord,
you were pleased to make glad the whole world,
grant, we beseech thee,
that through the intercession
of the Virgin Mary, his mother,
we may attain the joys of eternal life,
through the same Christ our Lord.

MEMORARE

Remember, most gracious Virgin Mary,
that never was it known that anyone
who fled to thy protection,
implored thy help,
or sought thy intercession,
was left unaided.
Inspired with this confidence,
I fly to thee,
O Virgin of virgins, my mother.
To thee I come; before thee I stand,
sinful and sorrowful.
Mother of the Word Incarnate,
despise not my petitions

but in thy mercy
hear and answer me.

HAIL, HOLY QUEEN

Hail, holy Queen, mother of mercy,
our life, our sweetness and our hope.
To thee do we cry,
poor banished children of Eve;
to thee we send up our sighs,
mourning and weeping
in this valley of tears.
Turn then, most gracious advocate,
thine eyes of mercy upon us,
and after this, our exile,
show unto us
the blessed fruit of thy womb, Jesus.
O clement, O loving, O kind Virgin Mary.

LITANY OF THE BLESSED VIRGIN MARY

We fly to your protection, holy Mother of God.
Despise not our petitions in our moments of need
but deliver us from all danger,
O ever glorious and blessed Virgin.

Lord, have mercy on us.
Christ, have mercy on us.
Lord, have mercy on us.
Christ, hear us.

Christ, graciously hear us.
God the Father of heaven, have mercy on us.
God the Son, Redeemer of the world, have mercy on us.
God the Holy Spirit, have mercy on us.
Holy Trinity, one God, have mercy on us.
Holy Mary, *pray for us.*
Holy Mother of God,...
Holy Virgin of virgins,...
Mother of Christ,...
Mother of divine grace,...
Mother most pure,...
Mother most chaste,...
Mother inviolate,...
Mother undefiled,...
Mother most amiable,...
Mother most admirable,...
Mother of good counsel,...
Mother of our Creator,...
Mother of our Savior,...
Virgin most prudent,...
Virgin most venerable,...
Virgin most renowned,...
Virgin most powerful,...
Virgin most merciful,...
Virgin most faithful,...
Mirror of justice,...

Seat of wisdom,...
Cause of our joy,...
Spiritual vessel,...
Vessel of honor,...
Singular vessel of devotion,...
Mystical rose,...
Tower of David,...
Tower of ivory,...
House of gold,...
Ark of the covenant,...
Gate of heaven,...
Morning star,...
Health of the sick,...
Refuge of sinners,...
Comforter of the afflicted,...
Help of Christians,...
Queen of angels,...
Queen of patriarchs,...
Queen of prophets,...
Queen of apostles,...
Queen of martyrs,...
Queen of confessors,...
Queen of virgins,...
Queen of all saints,...
Queen conceived without original sin,...
Queen of the most holy rosary,...
Queen of peace,...

Lamb of God, you take away the sins of the world, spare us, O Lord.
Lamb of God, you take away the sins of the world, graciously hear us, O Lord.

Lamb of God, you take away the sins of
 the world, have mercy on us.
Christ, hear us.
Christ, graciously hear us.

Pray for us, holy Mother of God:
That we may be made worthy of
 the promises of Christ.

Lord God,
may we your servants enjoy
continual health of mind and body;
through the glorious intercession
of Blessed Mary ever Virgin,
may we be freed from present sorrow
and enjoy eternal happiness,
through Jesus Christ, your Son, our Lord.

Known also as the Litany of Loreto

ROSARY

Joyful mysteries

First joyful mystery. The annunciation. The Word of God becomes flesh in the womb of the Virgin Mary.

Second joyful mystery. The visitation. Mary visits her cousin Elizabeth, mother of John the Baptist who will announce the coming of Christ.

Third joyful mystery. The nativity. Jesus is born in a stable in Bethlehem.

Fourth joyful mystery. The presentation. Jesus is presented in the Temple.

Fifth joyful mystery. The finding of our Lord in the Temple. Jesus is found by his parents among the teachers of God's law.

Sorrowful mysteries

First sorrowful mystery. The agony in the garden. Jesus prays that his Father's will be done.

Second sorrowful mystery. The scourging at the pillar. Pilate orders Jesus to be scourged.

Third sorrowful mystery. The crowning with thorns. The soldiers mock and insult Jesus, crowning him King of the Jews.

Fourth sorrowful mystery. The carrying of the cross. Jesus is led out of Jerusalem to die on the hill of Golgotha.

Fifth sorrowful mystery. The crucifixion. Jesus dies on the cross and is buried.

Glorious mysteries

First glorious mystery. The resurrection. Jesus is raised from the dead.

Second glorious mystery. The ascension. Jesus is taken up into the Father's glory.

Third glorious mystery. The descent of the Holy Spirit upon the apostles. As he had promised, Jesus sends the Spirit to his disciples.

Fourth glorious mystery. The assumption. Mary falls asleep in the Lord and enters her Son's heavenly glory.

Fifth glorious mystery. The crowning of Mary as Queen of heaven and earth. Mary becomes a special sign of the victory all share in Christ.

PRAYER AFTER THE ROSARY

God, thy only begotten Son,
by his life, death and resurrection,
has obtained for us the rewards of eternal life;
grant we beseech thee,
that meditating on these mysteries
of the holy rosary of Blessed Mary, his mother,
we may imitate what they contain
and obtain what they promise,
through Christ our Lord.

Devotions to the Saints and Angels

PRAYER TO ALL ANGELS AND SAINTS

Angels, archangels, thrones, dominions,
principalities, powers, heavenly virtues,
cherubim and seraphim;
all saints of God, holy men and women,
and especially you my patrons,
pray for us
that we may be worthy offerings to God,
to the praise and glory of his name,
for our welfare and that of all his holy people.

PRAYER TO SAINT JOSEPH

Blessed Joseph,
happy man whose privilege it was
not only to see and hear
the Lord whom many a king
longed to see, yet never saw,
and longed to hear,
yet never heard,
but even to carry him in your arms
and embrace him,
to clothe him and watch over him,
pray for us, blessed Joseph,
that we may be made worthy
of the promises of Christ.

LITTLE LITANY OF SAINT JOSEPH

Lord, have mercy on us.
Christ, have mercy on us.
Lord, have mercy on us.

Good Saint Joseph, pray for us.
Teach us to be honest, *Saint Joseph, pray for us.*
Teach us to be just,...
Teach us to be simple,...
Teach us to be kind,...
That we be not afraid of work,...
That we may respect all men and women,...
That we may have regard for the poor,...
That we may love our homes and families,...

O God,
you have given us Saint Joseph to be our model.
Make us like him,
simple, wise and kind,
through Christ your Son, our Lord.

Blanche Jennings Thompson

LITANY OF SAINT JOSEPH

Lord, have mercy on us.
Christ, have mercy on us.
Lord, have mercy on us.
Christ, hear us.

Christ, graciously hear us.
God the Father of heaven, have mercy on us.
God the Son, Redeemer of the world, have mercy on us.
God the Holy Spirit, have mercy on us.
Holy Trinity, one God, have mercy on us.

Holy Mary, pray for us.
Saint Joseph, *pray for us.*
Renowned offspring of David,...
Light of patriarchs,...
Spouse of the Mother of God,...
Chaste guardian of the Virgin,...
Foster-father of the Son of God,...
Diligent protector of Christ,...
Head of the Holy Family,...
Joseph most just,...
Joseph most chaste,...
Joseph most prudent,...
Joseph most strong,...
Joseph most obedient,...
Joseph most faithful,...
Mirror of patience,...
Lover of poverty,...
Model of workers,...
Glory of the life of the home,...
Guardian of virgins,...
Pillar of families,...
Solace of the wretched,...
Hope of the sick,...

Patron of the dying,...
Terror of demons,...
Protector of the holy Church,...

Lamb of God, you take away the sins of the world, spare us, O Lord.

Lamb of God, you take away the sins of the world, graciously hear us, O Lord.

Lamb of God, you take away the sins of the world, have mercy on us.

O God, in your unspeakable providence
you chose blessed Joseph
to be the spouse of the Virgin Mary.
As he has been our protector on earth,
may he also be our advocate in heaven,
through Christ our Lord.

LITTLE LITANY OF ANGELS

Lord, have mercy on us.
Christ, have mercy on us.
Lord, have mercy on us.
Holy angels of God, be with us always.
In all journeys, *holy angels be with us.*
In all our studies,...
In all our meditations,...
In all our labors,...
In all our pleasures,...
In all our temptations,...
In all our troubles,...
In all our sufferings,...

In all our good deeds,...
In the hour of danger,...
In the hour of trial,...
In the hour of death,...

Almighty and eternal God,
you send your holy messengers
to guard and protect us.
Grant that in their company
we may see and praise you for ever
in your Kingdom,
through Jesus Christ your Son.

LITANY OF THE SAINTS

Lord, have mercy on us.
Christ, have mercy on us.
Lord, have mercy on us.
Christ, hear us.
Christ, graciously hear us.

God our heavenly Father, have mercy on us.
God the Son, Redeemer of the world, have mercy on us.
God the Holy Spirit, have mercy on us.
Holy Trinity, one God, have mercy on us.

Holy Mary, *pray for us.*
Mother of God,...
Virgin of virgins,...
Saint Michael,...
Saint Gabriel,...
Saint Raphael,...

All you angels and archangels,...
All you blessed spirits,...
Saint John the Baptist,...
Saint Joseph,...
All you patriarchs and prophets,...
Saint Peter,...
Saint Paul,...
Saint Andrew,...
Saint James,...
Saint John,...
Saint Thomas,...
Saint James,...
Saint Philip,...
Saint Bartholomew,...
Saint Matthew,...
Saint Simon,...
Saint Jude,...
Saint Matthias,...
Saint Barnabas,...
Saint Luke,...
Saint Mark,...
All you holy apostles and evangelists,...
All you blessed disciples of the Lord,...
All you holy innocents,...
Saint Stephen,...
Saint Lawrence,...
Saint Fabian and Saint Sebastian,...
Saint John and Saint Paul,...
Saint Cosmas and Saint Damian,...
Saint Gervase and Saint Protase,...
All you holy martyrs,...

Saint Gregory,...
Saint Ambrose,...
Saint Augustine,...
Saint Jerome,...
Saint Athanasius,...
Saint Basil,...
Saint Martin,...
Saint Nicholas,...
All you holy bishops and confessors,...
All you holy doctors,...
Saint Anthony,...
Saint Benedict,...
Saint Bernard,...
Saint Francis and Saint Dominic,...
Saint Francis Xavier,...
Saint John Vianney,...
All you holy priests and ministers,...
All you holy monks and hermits,...
Saint Mary Magdalene,
Saint Perpetua and Saint Felicity,...
Saint Catherine,...
Saint Anastasia,...
Saint Teresa,...
All you holy virgins and widows,...
All you holy saints of God,...

Be merciful, O Lord; graciously hear us, O Lord.
From all evil, *deliver us, O Lord.*
From all sin,...
From thy anger,...

From sudden and unforeseen death,...
From hatred and ill will,...
From the spirit of immorality,...
From lightning and storm,...
From earthquake,...
From pestilence, famine and war,...
From everlasting death,...
By your holy incarnation,...
By your coming to us,...
By your birth,...
By your baptism and holy fasting,...
By your passion and cross,...
By your death and burial,...
By your holy resurrection,...
By your wonderful ascension,...
By your gift of the Holy Spirit, our Comforter,...
On the day of judgment,...
We are sinners, *we beg you, hear us.*
That you will spare us,...
That you will forgive us,...
That you will bring us to true repentance,...
That you will govern and protect your Church,...
That you will protect in holiness the Pope and all those in sacred orders,...
That you will humble the enemies of your Church,...
That you will give peace and concord to all rulers,...

That you will give peace and unity to all Christians,...
That your light might shine on all people,...
That you would strengthen and protect us in your service,...
That you would raise our minds to heaven,...
That you would reward all our benefactors with eternal blessings,...
That you would deliver us, our families, friends and benefactors from everlasting death,...
That you would increase and protect the fruits of the earth,...
That you would give eternal rest to all the faithful departed,...
That it may please you to hear us,...
Son of God,...

Lamb of God, you take away the sins of the world, spare us, O Lord.
Lamb of God, you take away the sins of the world, graciously hear us, O Lord.
Lamb of God, you take away the sins of the world, have mercy on us.
Christ, hear us.
Christ, graciously hear us.

Prayers for the Church

CHRIST'S PRIESTLY PRAYER

Father,
we make ours the prayer of your Son
before his hour of glory.
We believe you sent him,
and that in him we belong to you.
Let us grow in knowledge of you,
the only true God,
and your Son, Jesus Christ.
That our lives may be your glory on earth,
help us to accomplish the work
you have given us to do in Christ.
Keep us, your children, true to your name,
that we may be one like you and your Son.
You send us in your Son into the world —
consecrate us with him in truth
so that, one in you and the Son,
the world may believe you sent us.
Father, let us always abide in Christ
that we may see the glory you have given him
from all eternity.
Make your name known to us and through us,
that your love for the Son be in us
and that he live in us for ever.

Based on John 17

PRAYER FOR VOCATIONS

(1)

God our Father,
it is your will that all people be saved
and know your truth.
Send workers into your harvest
that the Gospel may be preached
to every creature and to all people.
Called forth by your word and your sacraments,
may we all advance in the way of salvation,
through Christ your Son, our Lord.

(2)

Father, you have called your people
to be the sacrament of salvation
for all the world.
Make us feel more urgently the call
to work for the salvation of all,
so that all people may be one in you.
Inspire us to continue the saving work of Christ
everywhere in this world,
for he is our Lord,
who lives and reigns with you for ever.

LITANY FOR PEACE

In peace let us pray to the Lord.
Lord, have mercy on us.

For peace from on high
and for our salvation,
let us pray to the Lord.
Lord, have mercy on us.

For the peace of the whole world,
for the welfare of all God's holy churches
and for their unity,
let us pray to the Lord.
Lord, have mercy on us.

For our God-loving Pope *N.* and bishop *N.*,
for all priests and deacons,
for all ministers and God's people,
let us pray to the Lord.
Lord, have mercy on us.

For the government of our country,
for all its institutions and its defenders,
let us pray to the Lord.
Lord, have mercy on us.

For help in all difficulties
and aid in the midst of adversity,
let us pray to the Lord.
Lord, have mercy on us.

For this city/village,
for every city, village and country,
and for the faithful who dwell within them,

let us pray to the Lord.
Lord, have mercy on us.

For good weather,
abundant fruits of the earth
and peaceful times,
let us pray to the Lord.
Lord, have mercy on us.

For all travellers, for the sick,
the suffering and prisoners,
and for the salvation of all people,
let us pray to the Lord.
Lord, have mercy on us.

For deliverance from all distress,
poverty and violence,
let us pray to the Lord.
Lord, have mercy on us.

Help us, save us, have mercy on us
and keep us, O God, in your grace.
Lord, have mercy on us.

Remembering our most holy,
most pure, most blessed and glorious Lady,
the Mother of God and ever-virgin Mary,
and all the saints,
let us commend ourselves,
one another
and our lives to Christ, our Lord.
To you, O Lord.

For all glory, honor and adoration are
yours,

Father, Son and Holy Spirit,
now and for ever.

From vespers of the Old Slavonic rite

TEACHING OF THE APOSTLES

We thank you, Father,
for the holy vine of David your servant
which you revealed to us through Jesus your Son.

Glory to you for ever.

We thank you, Father,
for the life and knowledge
which you sent us through Jesus your Son.

Glory to you for ever.

As the grain for our bread
was once scattered over the hills,
and now has been gathered and made one,
so may your Church throughout the world be one
and gathered together in your Kingdom.

Through Jesus Christ
glory and power are yours now and for ever.

We thank you, holy Father,
for your sacred name
which you have planted within us,
and for the knowledge, faith and immortality
you give us through Jesus Christ your Son.

Glory to you for ever.

Almighty Lord, you have made all things
to the glory of your name.
You give us food and drink
for our thankful enjoyment,
and you give us spiritual food and drink
for eternal life through your Son.
We thank you above all things,
you are all-powerful.

Glory to you for ever.

Lord, remember your Church.
Deliver us from evil;
teach us to love you perfectly.
You call your people to be holy;
gather us from all the world
into the Kingdom you have promised.

Glory and power are yours, now and for ever.

May your grace come; the world passes on.
Hosanna! God of David.
Come, Lord Jesus!

Known also as the Didache

Prayers in Times of Difficulty

BEATITUDES

Blessed are the poor in spirit;
theirs is the Kingdom of heaven.
Blessed are the gentle;
they shall inherit the earth.
Blessed are those who mourn;
they shall be comforted.
Blessed are those who hunger and thirst for righteousness:
they shall be satisfied.
Blessed are the merciful;
they shall have mercy shown them.
Blessed are the pure in heart;
they shall see God.
Blessed are the peacemakers;
they shall be called children of God.
Blessed are those who are persecuted in the cause of righteousness;
theirs is the Kingdom of heaven.
Blessed are you when people abuse you
and persecute you
and speak all kinds of calumny against you
on my account.
Rejoice and be glad,
for your reward will be great in heaven.

Matthew 5:1-12

SERENITY PRAYER

God, grant me the serenity
to accept the things
I cannot change;
courage to change
the things I can;
and wisdom
to know the difference.

PRAYER OF ST. FRANCIS

Lord, make me an instrument of your peace.
Where there is hatred, let me sow love;
where there is injury, pardon;
where there is doubt, faith;
where there is despair, hope;
where there is darkness, light;
and where there is sadness, joy.

Divine Master,
grant that I may not so much seek
to be consoled as to console,
to be understood as to understand,
to be loved as to love.

For it is in giving that we receive,
in pardoning that we are pardoned,
and in dying that we are born to eternal life.

LITTLE LITANY OF PRAISE

Lord, have mercy on us.
Christ, have mercy on us.
Lord, have mercy on us.
Lord God, we offer you our thanks.
For the gift of life, *we thank you, O God.*
For work and rest,...
For family and friends,...
For the warmth of the sun,...
For the cooling rain,...
For the moon and the stars,...
For the beauty of trees,...
For the loveliness of flowers,...
For the happiness of music,...
For the comforts of religion,...
For our special gifts and graces,...
For all our sorrows,...
For all your loving kindness,...

Almighty and eternal God,
grant that we may never forget to love you,
to adore you,
and to praise you in joy and in sorrow
all our lives long.

Blanche Jennings Thompson

DE PROFUNDIS

Out of the depths I call to you, Lord.
O Lord, listen to my cry.

Be attentive
to the sound of my pleading.

If you, Lord, note all our offences,
who then, O Lord, could stand?
But with you is forgiveness,
for which we revere you.

I wait for the Lord, my soul awaits;
I hope in his word.
My soul waits for the Lord,
more than watchmen wait for dawn,
more than watchmen awaiting the dawn.

Israel, hope in the Lord,
for with the Lord there is mercy
and generous redemption.
It is he who redeems Israel
from all their sins.

Psalm 129 (130)

MISERERE

Have mercy on me, God, in your kindness.
In your merciful goodness blot out my
offences.
Wash me clean from my wickedness,
cleanse me from my sin.

For I acknowledge my faults,
my sin is always before me.
Against you only have I sinned;
I have done what is evil in your sight.

Your judgment on me is just,
your sentence blameless.
You know I was born guilty,
conceived in sin.

You desire truth in the depths of my being,
teach me wisdom of heart.
Purify me with hyssop, I shall be clean;
wash me, I shall be whiter than snow.

Fill me with joy and gladness;
let my broken bones rejoice.
Hide your face from my sins
and blot out my offences.

Create in me a clean heart, God;
put an upright spirit within me.
Cast me not out of your presence;
deprive me not of your Holy Spirit.

Restore to me the joy of salvation,
make my spirit willing;
then I will teach transgressors your ways
and sinners will return to you.

Deliver me from death, God my Savior;
my tongue shall sing your righteousness.
Lord, open my lips
and my mouth shall praise you.

You take no delight in sacrifices;
burnt offerings do not please you.
The sacrifice of God is a broken heart;
you do not scorn a broken, contrite heart.

In your graciousness show favor to Zion;
rebuild the walls of Jerusalem.
Then you will delight in right sacrifice,
burnt offerings and whole oblations,
when they offer young bulls on your altar.

Psalm 50 (51)

PSALM OF OLD AGE

In you, Lord, I seek refuge;
let me not be put to shame.
In your righteousness, deliver me, rescue
me;
turn your ear to me and save me.

Be a rock of refuge for me,
a strong fortress to save me,
for you are my fortress and rock.

Rescue me, my God, from the hand of the
wicked,
from the grasp of the pitiless and unjust.
For you, Lord, are my hope,
my trust, from the days of my youth.

On you I have leaned from my birth,
you brought me forth from my mother's
womb —
you are my constant praise.

I have become a fearful omen to many,
but you are my refuge.
My mouth is filled with your praise;
I shall sing your glory all day long.

Cast me not off in the time of old age;
do not forsake me as my strength fails.

For my enemies speak about me,
watching me and conspiring.
They say, "God has forsaken him.
Seize him, take him.
No one will save him."

God, do not be far from me;
O God, hasten to help me.
Let my accusers be shamed and
confounded;
let those who seek my hurt know
what scorn and disgrace mean.

But my hope shall be constant;
I will praise you more and more.
My mouth shall speak of your salvation,
all day long tell of your righteousness,
although it surpasses all words.

I will begin with the mighty deeds of God,
declaring the righteousness that is yours
alone.
God, you have taught me from my youth,
and to this day I proclaim your deeds.

Now that I am old and gray-headed,
do not forsake me, God.
Let me show the strength of your arm
to the coming generations,
your might to those yet to come.

Your righteousness, Lord, reaches the
heavens;
great are the things you have done.
God, who is like you?

You have sent me misery and pain,
but you will revive me again;
from the depths of the earth
you will raise me to life.
You will increase my blessings,
comfort me again.

So I will praise you with the harp,
for your faithfulness, my God.
I will sing to you with the lute,
Holy One of Israel.

My lips will shout for joy;
I will sing your praises,
for you rescue my soul.

My tongue speaks of your righteous help
all day long,
while shame and disgrace
await those whose aim is to hurt me.

Psalm 70 (71)

Prayers for the Dead and Dying

CHRIST'S PROMISE

Jesus, remember us in your kingdom.
For you promised the dying thief,
"This day you will be with me in
paradise."

Luke 23:42-43

ETERNAL REST

Eternal rest,
grant unto him/her/them, O Lord,
and let perpetual light shine upon
him/her/them.

May he/she/they and all the faithful
departed
through the mercy of God
rest in peace.

NUNC DIMITTIS

Now, Master,
you can let your servant go in peace,
just as you promised;
for my eyes have seen the salvation
which you prepared
for all peoples to see,
a light to enlighten the nations,
and the glory of your people, Israel.

Luke 2:29-32

LITANY FOR THE DEAD

In peace let us pray to the Lord.
Lord, have mercy on us.

For God's servant *N.* and his/her blessed repose,
let us pray to the Lord.
Lord, have mercy on us.

That all his/her sins be forgiven,
let us pray to the Lord.
Lord, have mercy on us.

That he/she be with Abraham, Isaac and Jacob,
let us pray to the Lord.
Lord, have mercy on us.

That he/she be with the living,
in the land of peace,
with all the saints and the just,
let us pray to the Lord.
Lord, have mercy on us.

That he/she stand uncondemned
before the judgment seat of Christ,
let us pray to the Lord.
Lord, have mercy on us.

That he/she inherit
the immortal Kingdom of heaven,
let us pray to the Lord.
Lord, have mercy on us.

That he/she partake of the ceaseless gladness
enjoyed by the saints from all ages,
let us pray to the Lord.
Lord, have mercy on us.

For deliverance
from all distress, poverty and violence,
let us pray to the Lord.
Lord, have mercy on us.

O Lord, help us, save us,
have mercy on us and keep us in your grace.
Lord, have mercy on us.

Remembering our most holy, most pure,
most blessed and glorious Lady,
the Mother of God and ever-virgin Mary,
and all the saints,
let us commend ourselves,
one another
and our lives to Christ our Lord.
To you, O Lord.

For you are the resurrection,
the life and the peace
of your departed servant, O Christ our Lord,
and we give you glory with your eternal Father
and the most holy and blessed Spirit of life,
now and for ever.

God of spirit and flesh,
you conquered death and destroyed evil,
giving life to the world;
grant peace to your departed servant *N.*,
keep him/her free from all pain and sorrow.

Because you love the people whom you have made,
forgive all his/her sins
of thought, word and deed,
for no one is without sin,
only you, O God.
Your truth lasts for eternity,
and our eternal life is your Word,
Jesus Christ,
who lives and reigns with you for ever.

Old Slavonic service for the dead

MAY SAINTS AND ANGELS LEAD YOU

Come to his/her rescue, saints of God;
run out to meet him/her, angels of the Lord.

Welcome him/her;
lead him/her into the presence of the Most High.

May Christ, who called you, receive you.
May the angels lead you to Abraham's bosom.
Lead him/her into the presence of the Most High.

Eternal rest grant him/her, O Lord,
and let perpetual light shine upon him/her.
Lead him/her into the presence of the Most High.

To you, Lord, we commend
your servant.
Dead to this world, may he/she live unto you.
In your merciful kindness, forgive whatever sins
he/she has committed out of human weakness.

Grant, O God, that while we lament
the departure of your servant *N.*,
we may always remember
that we will follow him/her.
Give us the grace to prepare
for that last hour by a good life.
May we not be surprised
by a sudden and unexpected death,
but may we be ever watching,
and thus, when you call,
may we enter eternal glory,
through Christ our Lord.

LITANY FOR THE DYING

Lord, have mercy on him/her.
Christ, have mercy on him/her.
Lord, have mercy on him/her.

Holy Mary, *pray for him/her.*
All you holy angels and archangels,...
Holy Abel,...
All you choirs of the righteous,...
Holy Abraham,...
Saint John the Baptist,...
Saint Joseph,...
All you holy patriarchs and prophets,...
Saint Peter,...
Saint Paul,...
Saint Andrew,...
Saint John,...
All you holy apostles and evangelists,...
All you holy disciples of our Lord,...
All you holy innocents,...
Saint Stephen,...
Saint Lawrence,...
All you holy martyrs,...
Saint Sylvester,...
Saint Gregory,...
Saint Augustine,...
All you holy bishops and confessors,...
Saint Benedict,...
Saint Francis,...
Saint Camillus,...
Saint John of God,...

All you holy monks and hermits,...
Saint Mary Magdalene,...
Saint Lucy,...
All you holy virgins and widows,...
All you men and women, saints of God, intercede for him/her.

Lord, be merciful to him/her; spare him/her, O Lord.
Lord, be merciful to him/her; set him/her free, O Lord.
In your mercy, *free him/her, O Lord.*
From your wrath,...
From the danger of death,...
From an evil death,...
From the pains of hell,...
From all evil,...
From the power of the Evil One,...
By your nativity,...
By your passion and cross,...
By your death and burial,...
By your glorious resurrection,...
By your wonderful ascension,...
By the grace of the Holy Spirit, the Comforter,...
On the day of judgment,...
We sinners, we beseech you, hear us.
That you would spare him/her, we beseech you, hear us.
Lord, have mercy on him/her.

Christ, have mercy on him/her.
Lord, have mercy on him/her.

Go forth, O Christian, out of this world,
in the name of the Father Almighty
who created you;
in the name of Jesus Christ,
the Son of the living God,
who suffered for you;
in the name of the Holy Spirit,
who sanctified you;
in the name of the holy and glorious Mary,
virgin and Mother of God;
in the name of the angels, archangels,
thrones and dominions, cherubim and
seraphim;
in the name of the patriarchs and
prophets,
of the holy apostles and evangelists,
of the holy martyrs, confessors, monks and
hermits,
of the holy virgins
and of all the saints of God.
May you this day be in peace,
through Christ our Lord.

God of mercy and compassion,
in your loving kindness
you forgive the sins of those who repent.
Look with mercy on your servant *N.*,
free him/her from all sins.

Merciful Father,
heal what has been wounded through weakness
or through the snares of evil.
Let him/her share in the unity of the saints.
Have mercy, Lord, on his/her sufferings,
and grant him/her your forgiveness,
for you are our only hope,
through Christ our Lord.

4

Readings and Meditations for the Wayfarer

Now

LIVING WELL

You can do nothing about avoiding death, but you can do something about living well.

Saint Augustine

DO IT NOW

If with pleasure you are viewing
Any work someone is doing,
If you like them or you love them,
Tell them now.

More than fame and more than money
Is the comment kind and sunny
And the hearty, warm approval of a friend,
For it gives in life a savor,
It makes you stronger, braver,
And it gives you heart and courage to the end.

Author unknown

TOO PRECIOUS TO WASTE

I once was teaching a class. And I was trying to tell the kids not to waste time. I said to one kid, "How old are you?" He said, "Thirteen." I said, "How much longer do you think you're going to live?" He hadn't given it a thought. "Well, let's assume that you and I are going to live to be seventy-five years old. You have sixty-two more years in which to live. That's a lot of time. I'm seventy years old. I only have five more years left. Now, you little stinker, don't waste my time, it's too precious."

Rabbi Aaron Blumenthal,
Aging as a Spiritual Journey
by Eugene C. Bianchi, p. 248
Crossroad Publishing Company,
New York, ©1982

WE ARE NEVER FINISHED

The creative in us bespeaks our yearning for immortality, our struggle against death, the universal struggle between mortality and eternity. There are other reasons, but one of the greatest that keeps creative minds alive and flourishing until the moment of death — and that, often at a great age — is the knowledge that their work will outlive them. If for no other reason, our life on this earth cannot be final — we are never finished. Our productivity can go on for ever; hence we require an eternity to realize our creativity.

Trust in God... But Tie Your Camel
by Sister Sylvia McDonald, CND, p. 91
Novalis, Ottawa, ©1983

MAKING NOW COUNT

Much can be done in preparation for more meaningful older age. One thing is to be realistic and positive about the limits of physical life. Physical death is universal and but a heartbeat away from any one of us from infancy to actual death. It is a positive thing to take our mortality into our self-affirmation. To be physically mortal is a part of who we are. This need not be a "morbid" attitude taken with defeatist resignation. It can be salutary to see that as to physical life, all any of us has right now is now. Past and future have their proper places and importance, but in youth and older age we can try to make now count.

The Bible Speaks on Aging
by Frank Stagg, pp. 186-87
Broadman Press, Nashville, Tenn., ©1981

FINDING JOY

Many aging people make their lives unnecessarily hard because they are blind to the good things that God offers them at this stage of life, experiences that should be enjoyed.

Each person has to discover in his or her own way the joys of old age. For some it may be the grandchildren who become a source of delight and satisfaction. Others may develop a new interest in the enjoyment of art, music and literature, or they may experience a new pleasure in the splendor and beauty of God's creation. A healthy pride in the achievements of one's life will offer a feeling of satisfaction to many retired men and women. A growing number of older people are finding great profit in Bible classes.

The aging should make a positive effort to develop a sense of joy in making themselves unobtrusively available for others. They will be surprised how much joy there can be in the simple efforts of being kind to others and of being available for those who need them. Because the aging develop a more nuanced sensitivity and appreciation for kindness shown them, they are also able to be more sensitive to the needs of others and can find new delights in showing them personal attention and love.

God wants us to be joyful.

Adapted from
Growing Old and How to Cope with It
by Alfons Deeken, pp. 61-62
Paulist Press, New York, ©1972

PEOPLE AREN'T MADE FOR WORK

Our tradition — which insists that each day we must do something to prove again that we have the right to be here — is disastrous for many older people, for whom forced retirement or impairment means that they are no longer able to "produce." Many thus feel worthless. Work should be a joyous privilege, an open opportunity to anyone able to work. Older people should have the right not to work when work is no longer a positive factor for them. Older persons need to be assured of and to accept the right to be — to be themselves with security, dignity and meaning.

Work is not to be an end in itself, else one becomes a "workaholic." Work is proper as a means to serving other people and/or as personal fulfilment. Older people who can work and want to work should have the opportunity to work. Older people who want to rest from work should be privileged to do so with dignity and security. Persons were not made for work, but work has meaning as it contributes to human fulfilment.

Adapted from
The Bible Speaks on Aging,
Frank Stagg, p. 189

EVERY DAY IS GOD'S GIFT

Since life is a gift, living must be a stewardship. All of life is God's gift, not just its early years. Each phase of life has its burdens and opportunities, and later life is no exception. The question is how to fulfil the specific stewardship that devolves upon the aged. The first part of this stewardship is recognition that every day of life, not just the early or youthful days, is God's gift. All times are God's time. Unfortunately, many see and define the latter days as burden, not as adventure. As a result, they grow weary with the burden instead of rejoicing in the gift. Days are spent waiting in inactivity for life to end. Old minds atrophy from disuse. Aging hearts draw back from involvement, fearing that the strain may be too much, and are dwarfed. For those who accept each new day as a divine gift to be used, life is renewed.

Adapted from
"Theology for Aging" by Carl G. Howie,
Spiritual Well-Being of the Elderly, p. 67,
National Intra-Decade Conference
on Spiritual Well-Being of the Elderly,
edited by James A. Thorson and Thomas C. Cook, Jr.
Charles C. Thomas, Springfield, Ill., ©1980

PAST — THAT'S WHAT THE WORD MEANS

How marvellous that in life the past can be just that. The word "past" does mean something that is over; we need not return to it unless we choose. I know from experience that the past can continue to haunt us into the present and darken our hopes about the future. But it needn't be that way. We can have a future and a present, too, without the crippling cords of the past.

Before we can do that, though, I think two things must happen. First — and while this may sound like an oversimplification, I think it is not — we must let the past be the past.

Thank goodness we live in a world where time exists, where the past can be a past. I'm not sure it's always going to be like that. It's beyond my brain to grasp the concept of eternity, where there is only the present, where "time" as we know it is nonexistent. But for now, on earth, there is a past, present and future. Before we can truly live in the present and future, though, we must let go of the past. Yes, it's easier said than done, and there's no foolproof way of going about it. Part of the real cure comes from saying, "OK, that is the past, but thank God there's a future as well."

The second thing that must happen is that we come to the knowledge that the future, yes our future, is in the hands of a loving God who will act in our lives if we but ask him and let him.

The God that I know, as he was revealed to me in Jesus Christ, is the kind of God I can love, do love. He is the kind of God who can take a broken past and turn even that into a hope for the future. And I'm not talking about a future in some kind of "heaven," but one on this earth, in this body. It's fine to say the word "past" means just that. But how much better and more helpful to say, "Not only is the past behind you, but you can have a joyful future, which the past cannot contaminate, if you will put your trust in Jesus Christ." Psalm [29] 30:5 is very appropriate to this point: "Weeping may tarry for the night, but joy comes with the morning."

Adapted from
Joy Comes with the Morning; A Handbook of Christian Encouragement and Affirmation
by William M. Kinnaird, pp. 121-122
Word Books, Waco, Texas, 1980, ©1979

THANK GOD FOR WHAT'S LEFT

Thank God for what you have left. No, you cannot do what you did when you were young — never again. But, whatever it is, thank God for what you have left. You, too, have affliction somewhere? You have hurts, arthritis, bursitis, or all the rest? Thank God for what you have left; that he has given you strength and faith enough to go through with life. I have an ankle that I have to live with the rest of my life. Sometimes it bothers me so much that I cannot go without a cane. I have been in a wheelchair, and I have been on crutches. I have been in pain. It still pains me when I walk too far or stand too long. I can thank God, though, for what I have left, I can finally get where I am going. I may not get there fast, but I can still get there. Thank God that I have that left.

We aged and senior citizens have something else to be very thankful for. Most of us have false teeth. We used to have good teeth and had no toothache, had none of our teeth missing. Then they kept on coming out until we lost them all, and we had to buy some teeth. So we do not have those teeth that God gave us, we have bought teeth. But we can still eat. So, thank God you still have some teeth that you can eat with. We were having a testimony meeting not long ago, and different ones were getting up thanking God for what they had faced and one said, "I want to say just a word — I want to thank God for my teeth. You remember, Brother and Sister, the last time you saw me I didn't have no teeth, but I have my teeth now. Thank God for my teeth." Thank God for what you have left.

"An Affirmation of Life"
by Martin Luther King, Senior,
Spiritual Well-Being of the Elderly, p. 85

Aging

SPRING

It's always springtime in the heart that loves God.

Saint John Vianney

MANIFESTING THE LORD

He in whom we have died and in whom we have risen from the dead, lives and is manifested in every movement of our body and our spirit.

Pope Saint Leo I

BEING BORN AGAIN

Nicodemus can be born again, even when old (John 3:4). Probably no lesson from our studies is more urgent than this: change for the better may come at any stage in life, but the best time to get ready to be old is when one is yet young.

The Bible Speaks on Aging,
Frank Stagg, p. 183

OLD IS BEAUTIFUL

Peace with oneself is essential to any age. This means self-acceptance and self-affirmation. At any age, one should be open to growth and betterment, but there is a wholesome acceptance of oneself, "warts and all." This includes acceptance of one's age, whatever it is. There is good news for us all. It is all right to be young, and it is all right to be old! Just as it was a victory for black people when they and others came to recognize that "black is beautiful," so it is right for us to recognize that "old, too, can be beautiful!"

The Bible Speaks on Aging,
Frank Stagg, p. 189

FOREVER BEGINNING

God sees the old not as childish, but as what they have been and will be, his children. He makes allowances for the past and does not forget what the elderly sinner is too apt to forget, the circumstances of temptation, the pitfalls on the way to spiritual triumph. Looking back regretfully, I wonder why such a mistaken course, but God knows what my limitations were. On the other hand, it seems to me that he expects me to demand of myself the ultimate of which he and I know me to be capable. Some of my associates might excuse me from effort because of my years, and it is a temptation to avail myself of their leniency, but if I am gentle and firm with myself, I can continue the struggle for perfection.

"Continue" seems hardly the word for something forever beginning!

Towards Evening
by Mary Hope, p. 85
Sheed and Ward, London, 1956

BECOMING YOUNG IN SOUL

One of the most moving joys of old age is to be able to applaud the success of those who have taken our place. To see that our successors are doing better than we did, to note that the young people's achievements are surpassing our own: that is the subtle pleasure that comes to a soul that has suddenly risen to the wider viewpoint of the common good, and takes in the supernatural horizon of the greater glory of God. Now at last motives are purified.

A learned and perspicacious monk said in a talk to a religious order of women: "There is a purity of heart and a youthfulness of soul which we do not really understand till the years begin to weigh down on our shoulders. There is a purity and youthfulness of soul that does not really flower till the body loses its strength and more and more of our friends disappear. There are old people who are completely young in soul..."

It is the paradox of old age that it should bring purification and rejuvenation with it. It is so essential to be like little children to enter into the Kingdom of heaven.

The Lord Is Near
by Cardinal Paul-Marie Richaud, p. 17
Translated by Ronald Matthews
Geoffrey Chapman, London, 1958

SHARING THE HARVEST

Old age is the crowning point of earthly life, a time to gather in the harvest you have sown. It is a time to give of yourselves to others as never before.

Pope John Paul II
Vancouver, Canada, Sept. 19, 1984

GRANDPARENTS FORGIVE EASILY

We do indeed continue to harbor grudges as we grow old, and there are stubborn hatreds that yield with difficulty to the years, but many resentments seem to disappear with those who were the causes of them. The graves that open round us almost always swallow up the wrongs of those who angered us. When there is no longer the contact with them to excite feelings and distort motives, we can better appreciate what was positive about them. Our judgments are always near the truth

when we temper them with indulgence. Grandparents forgive easily and are friendly people to have things out with.

"Stay with us," the two disciples of Emmaus said to Christ. "It is toward evening, and it is far on in the day" (Luke 24:29). Is it not in the evening of life and when, from a human point of view, it is far on in the day, that the divine light begins to shine at its clearest?

Adapted from *The Lord Is Near,*
Paul-Marie Richaud, pp. 12-13

SACRED TASK FOR THE ELDERLY

The young of today are separated from the elders by World War II, and the inconceivably rapid developments of the postwar period: cultural, political, ideological. For those of us who predate even World War I, this difference is all the more noticeable.

Today's youth live in, and are living in, a world and a set of cultural standards that we gave them. Because of today's rapid changes, we are charged with the duty, and the privilege, to keep these standards clear and uncontaminated: this is the great responsibility of the older generation, and it is a privilege as well.

The elders could then permit themselves, for instance, certain liberties which, in our time, did not bring the immediate and devastating consequences that such indulgence does today. A bit of excess drinking, for instance, has a very different meaning for youth at the controls of a speeding automobile than it had for youth in more leisurely times, when the good old carriage horse would bring the somewhat confused driver home. It was the older people, not the young, who created the demoralizing urban conditions that still "breed" juvenile delinquency... If we frankly recognize these mistakes and their effect upon the younger generation, there still remains the great and sacred task of passing on to them the best that we have.

Reflections on Growing Old
by Father John LaFarge, SJ, pp. 60-61
Doubleday, Garden City, N.Y., ©1963

GIFTS AGE CAN GIVE

The passing of the years brings its frailties. You may be forced to give up activities that you once enjoyed. Your limbs may not seem as agile as they used to be. Your memory and your eyesight may refuse to give service. And so the world may cease to be familiar — the world of your family, the world around you, the world you once knew. Even the Church, which you have loved for so long, may seem strange to many of you as she goes forward in this period of renewal. Yet despite changes and any weaknesses you may feel, you are of great value to all. Society needs you and so does the Church...

We need your experience and your insights. We need the faith which has sustained you and continues to be your light. We need your example of patient waiting and trust. We need to see in you that mature love which is yours, that love which is the fruit of your lives lived in both joys and sorrows. And yes, we need your wisdom for you can offer assurance in times of uncertainty. You can be an incentive to live according to the higher values of the spirit.

Pope John Paul II
Vancouver, Canada, Sept. 18, 1984

PREROGATIVE OF AGE

Age is the time for some degree of contemplation. I am not speaking of mystical rapture, but rather of the thoughtful, peaceful enjoyment of nature, of art, of the sequence of human events, of insight into those relations and connections of things that so often means so much more than the individual objects themselves.

In the Oriental paintings — Chinese or Japanese — you do not see young people seated in meditation near a waterfall. The contemplative hermit is aged, quite as a matter of course. This is age's prerogative, to be seated near the roaring stream of life, and relate it to the imperishable stream of one's own life within one.

Adapted from *Reflections of Growing Old*,
John LaFarge, pp. 82-83

ENJOYING THE PEACE OF EVENING

The evening of life is very like the peaceful last hours of daylight in the country. The farmer, sitting on a seat with its back to the house, tranquilly watches people coming back to the village and exchanges with them remarks that are poles removed from the hectic conversations of the city bar or the hard-hitting arguments of the union meeting. What is he thinking of as he rests after a hard day's work? He has his worries about the crops, and about the weather in the next few days. Memories of his older sons, who are possibly far away, may haunt him too. But the sight of the children playing under his eyes calms him and takes his mind off his cares. The cool of the evening relaxes him. He looks back over the work that has been done since the season began. He thinks of what he has still got to clear and to cut, to pick and to gather in. He leaves all that for the days ahead.

Every life should end in peace like that. Possibly it has not been sufficiently noticed that Christ kept the affectionate phrases in which he wished peace to his apostles for his last conversations with them.

The Lord wants our declining years to be really a period of moral and spiritual ascent, in which we go forward smoothly, as when a mountaineer's steps become even slower and more regular as he tackles the last few feet of the peak. And from the top, every perspective is simplified. The feature that looked so big down in the plain, has been levelled out. We find an all-embracing view, purer air, a deeper solemnity, but also a greater luminousness in the countryside; we are caught up in a sort of harmony which fills mind and body alike.

The Lord Is Near,
Paul-Marie Richaud, pp. 28-29

Happiness

BEING THANKFUL

No duty is more urgent than that of returning thanks.

Saint Ambrose

LIFE'S SONG

Don't let your life misrepresent your song. Sing with your voice. Sing with your heart. Sing with your mouth. But especially sing with your whole life.

Saint Augustine

EVERYBODY'S SOMEBODY

Redemption comes through Jesus Christ, who has made each a somebody. That is the basic affirmation of the Gospel. Those whom others call "nobodies," nonpersons, have become "new creations," somebodies, in Jesus Christ. God does not change this process with age.

"Theology for Aging" by Carl G. Howie,
Spiritual Well-Being of the Elderly, p. 67

ACCEPTING OURSELVES

Another factor in growing old meaningfully is the willingness to accept the God-given right to be oneself. Life is gift, and the right to be oneself is gift. We do not have to earn the right to be. We had no-

thing to do with being born into the world. We are not responsible for being here, but in being here we are responsible. One of our responsibilities is to accept ourselves and our right to be.

The Bible Speaks on Aging,
Frank Stagg, p. 188

ENJOYING PRECIOUS TIME

Redemption involves recognition of dependence on God and on others for life. It also requires coming to grips with mortality and other limits set on all of human life. As it relates to age, redemption allows persons to live with unfinished projects and unanswered questions. It is, then, possible to admit the reality of death and the incompleteness of life. There is a lessening of anxiety about time running out and greater joy in the preciousness of remaining time.

"Theology for Aging" by Carl G. Howie,
Spiritual Well-Being of the Elderly, pp. 66-67

SURVIVORS OR ENJOYERS?

We may have the assurance of life beyond physical death, a basic Christian assurance, and that in itself should be a sustaining factor; but life should have

meaning here and now. Fullness of life is possible now, transcending the fluctuations of physical factors. The fruit of the Spirit is love, joy, peace, patience, kindness, goodness, faith, gentleness, and self-control (Galatians 5:22). These are the qualities which can enter into a life and give it direction and meaning. These qualities cannot be imposed upon us, but they are there for us if we are open to God and these qualities. Such qualities can make the difference between being enjoyers or just survivors or casualties in the later years.

The Bible Speaks on Aging,
Frank Stagg, p. 187

PRIORITY NUMBER ONE

Different people regularly see the same thing in different ways.

A mother, hearing a crash in the kitchen, exclaimed, "Oh, Debby, not more dishes!" Debby's reply: "No, mother, fewer dishes!"

And so it is through all the range of human likes and dislikes: what one person likes, someone else disdains or is completely indifferent to it, whether it be politics, periodicals, pollution, promotions, people. But see the mistake right there! We listed people last.

Actually, it's only because there are people that things have any relevancy.

So, in an accurate perspective it's people who are the number one priority. It is people who are most important — people... you and me and other people, with our hopes and dreams, our wondrous potential, our aspirations and abilities, our uniqueness. It is only because of us, people, that things take on meaning.

William O'Meara

WHAT MAKES US HAPPY?

The Beatitudes in the Sermon on the Mount are highly instructive as to factors which largely determine the quality of life, in youth or old age. Jesus declared "blessed" or "happy" persons characterized by such qualities as meekness, hunger and thirst for righteousness, mercifulness, purity of heart, peacemaking, and the willingness to suffer for the sake of Christ and of what is right. The list is not exhaustive, but it points out the direction of meaningful life. If one wants to grow old gracefully, with beauty and power, these are among the qualities which must be best built into life, and the earlier the better.

Nothing has so much to do with the quality of life and its fulfilment, whether young or old, as the principle which Jesus made primary. If we try to save ourselves, we self-destruct; if we are willing to lose ourselves to God and other people, we find life (John 12:25). Like a grain of wheat, one must "die" to "live" (verse 24). To be selfish, turned in upon oneself, guarantees failure. Nothing so damages human existence and makes the later years emptier or more miserable than garden-variety selfishness. On the other hand, just look around at the older people whose lives are radiant in power and beauty. They are not selfish people. They are people who have found life by giving it to God and to the service of other people.

The Bible Speaks on Aging,
Frank Stagg, pp. 187-88

Suffering

ENDURING

Nothing great was ever done without much enduring.

Saint Catherine of Siena

PRAYING WITH GROANS

The best prayers often have more groans than words.

John Bunyan

EYES ON GOD

Believe me, by God's help we shall advance more by contemplating the divinity than by keeping our eyes fixed on ourselves.

Saint Teresa of Avila

SHARING PAIN

Shared pain is somehow like shared bread — it brings its participants closer to each other...

Towards Evening,
Mary Hope, p. 105

COMFORTING THE SORROWFUL

Occasionally, we have the privilege of letting another ease a troubled mind by talking to us. To listen quietly in union with our Lord is to share the habitual charity of

God, who forever listens to us all... The young and the strong can nurse the sick; but we, feeble and weary, can comfort the sorrowful, for we, knowing sorrow, know sympathy.

Towards Evening,
Mary Hope, p. 104

PRAYER OF THE AFFLICTED

The Blessed Virgin must take particular delight in the rosaries of the old. The rosary is well-fitted to the capacity of the afflicted. No need to hear, or see, or speak...

Towards Evening,
Mary Hope, p. 142

COPING WITH SUFFERING

I will never forget one evening in a New York hospital, when an elderly lady suffering from cancer explained to me what the following two passages from Saint Paul meant to her: "If we are afflicted it is for your salvation" (2 Corinthians 1:6), and "Now I rejoice in my sufferings for your sake" (Colossians 1:24). "These two Scripture texts," she said, "give a profound meaning to my sickness. I can offer my sufferings for other people and in this way help them to achieve salvation. Confined to this hospital bed, I still can help other people to come to the faith and to enjoy the hope and joy that Jesus Christ bestows on those who believe in him. At the same time, this slow dying has become easier for me since I began to see a meaning in suffering."

The experience of suffering in old age takes on its deepest meaning when it is seen and accepted in the agony of Christ in Gethsemani and on the cross. The whole life of the Christian is a walking in the footsteps of the Master, but it would seem that for many Christians it is only in old age that they are admitted to share fully in the agony of Christ's last days on earth.

Growing Old and How to Cope with It,
Alfons Deeken, pp. 58-59

GOD REVEALED

The life of sacrifice and the life of charity are a manifestation of God — who is specially present in the one who suffers and the one who comes to help. It is as if God who loves comes to the aid of God who suffers. But then isn't it the same God who declares, "You are my beloved Son," as cries from the cross, "Why have you abandoned me?"

Translated from Brother Bernard Marie, OFS
L'Ange de Tobie, p. 240
Éditions du Chalet, Paris, ©1985

HARD LESSON OF REDEMPTION

The disciples of Emmaus had not grasped the fundamental meaning of existence, the basic policy of the divine government of the world. They refused to admit that the Messiah, in whom they had placed their trust, could have undergone the ignominious punishment and died on a cross. Jesus revealed to them what is at once the mystery of his existence and of ours:

> Was it not to be expected that the Christ should undergo these sufferings, and enter so into his glory?" (Luke 24:26)

We have such confidence in life, we are so much inclined to relate everything to ourselves, and to think of ourselves as superior and indispensable beings, that it seems to us unthinkable that we should have to suffer and lose our importance. It can sometimes be said of those who are growing old that, when misfortune and incapacity overtake them,

> Jesus began to make it known to them that the Son of Man must be much ill-used and be rejected. (Mark 8:31)

The lesson is a hard one, there is no disguising it. But it is an encouraging lesson too. Since such is the law of redemption, since this is the great recipe for winning over the heart of God, since it is so much more necessary to purchase than it is to perform, we shall finally know the genuine feeling of gaining what we had so much longed for.

The Lord Is Near,
Paul-Marie Richaud, pp. 16-17

PRAYER OF THE HUMBLE

I asked God for strength, that I might achieve. I was made weak, that I might learn humbly to obey.

I asked for health, that I might do greater things. I was given infirmity, that I might do better things.

I asked for riches, that I might be happy. I was given poverty, that I might be wise.

I asked for all things, that I might enjoy life. I was given life, that I might enjoy all things.

I got nothing that I asked for, but everything I had hoped for. Despite myself, my prayers were answered. I among all people am most richly blessed.

Anonymous soldier,
American Civil War

THE LAST INVOCATION

At the last, tenderly,
From the walls of the powerful fortressed
house,
From the clasp of the knitted locks, from
the keep of the well-closed doors,
Let me be wafted.

Let me glide noiselessly forth;
With the key of softness unlock the locks
— with a whisper,
Set ope the doors, O Soul.

Tenderly — be not impatient,
(Strong is your hold, O mortal flesh.
Strong is your hold, O Love.)

Walt Whitman

Faith

BECOMING CHRIST

The Word of God, Jesus Christ, on account of his great love for humanity, became what we are in order to make us what he is himself.

Saint Irenaeus

PREPARING FOR ETERNITY

I asked a very old and holy confessor what one must do to be holy in old age. "What do you expect to do throughout eternity?" he inquired. "To adore God, I hope." "Begin now," he counselled, and added, "and be like a little child."

Towards Evening,
Mary Hope, p. 34

PRAYER NEEDS NO WORDS

My prayer is so often a dumb prayer, simply stupid stillness, no mental activity, or, if there is any, a series of silly distractions. Yet it is serene, for I am entirely dependent on God, and now know that I am. He does not ask labored meditation or unlabored ecstasy; what he asks is my "fiat" [let it be done to be me], my union of my will with his. This prayer is marked by willing, peaceful surrender to God's choice. It is the prayer of the old. It asks no delight, no enlightenment. Were it not wordless, it would be expressed in the words of Christ: "Father, into thy hands I commend my spirit."

Towards Evening,
Mary Hope, pp. 52-53

AS MEMORY FAILS

Memory may sometimes fail us over recent events. But our oldest memories are still there and crowd in upon us. The frets of life grow blurred. Our glance may not be so keen, but it is less subject to distractions. It is on the core of our deepest convictions that we must stand fast then.

It will do no harm if we simplify our devotions. They will seem to us to have lost their richness. It is impossible to keep up the same effort of concentration or to repeat the same prayers and the same exercises. The spiritual life of the sick soon reduces itself to an act of offering.

When that happens, we must not think that it represents a retreat or a falling off. The soul that empties itself of itself is giving itself up, and that is the last filial disposition of the Christian: the supreme and total conformity to the divine will that is as comforting as it is spiritual and efficacious.

The Lord Is Near,
Paul-Marie Richaud, p. 29

HUMANITY'S COMMON LOT

The Second Vatican Council has emphasized for us a world of mutual help that over the years has been greatly neglected: that of friendly intercourse with people of other faiths, who share with us belief in God and some of our deepest religious and moral convictions. If more of that sharing had been done in the past, the world's religious forces would not be as they are today, a prey to their own misunderstandings. I am not speaking of honest differences, but of those human weaknesses that frank and friendly conversation can minimize, even if it cannot abolish.

For peace and happiness in those latter years let me remember that the phenomena that trouble me — the diminishments and burdens proper to old age — are not something that has just happened to me personally; they are the common lot of mankind, for better or worse, and thus form a meeting ground for all other human beings. Still more is it vital for me to understand that through the medium of this commonly shared human experience, interpreted and supported by a God-given and steadfast hope, I come into closer contact, if I so wish, with the development of a new life: the life of divinely given charity, the vitality of the Creator himself imparted to his creatures! imparted, that is to say, as the life of the vine is imparted to its branches.

Reflections on Growing Old,
John LaFarge, p. 61

SEASON FOR CONTEMPLATION

Two habits are especially important to me now: (1) the practice of the presence of God, keeping myself, as nearly as possible, mindful of him and united to him day and night; (2) the frequent reading of, and meditation on, the Gospels and the life of our Lord rather than any other books of devotion, because their teachings are the spiritual food on which the contemplative must depend; and old age, to be holy, must almost necessarily be a season of contemplation... to know the God whom we adore, we read the life of Jesus Christ.

Towards Evening,
Mary Hope, p. 6

CALL TO PRAYER

Where is the living God of Abraham, Isaac and Jacob?

The Scriptures have become a stony tomb, sealed against our entry. Ages of religious experience, God's very word, lie buried therein, usually in deathly silence, at most in muted, undecipherable sound. Like the Galilean women at dawn on the third day we ask: Who will roll away the stone for us? Who will transform that sound into a living word?

Is it the voice of the prophet which has grown weak? Or is it our hearing which has grown dull? Can it be that Thomas à Kempis has a message for us?

> Whoever wishes to understand and fully savor the words of Christ must seek to conform his life to that of Christ.

O God, that we may hear! "Lord, teach us to pray" (Luke 11:1).

Adapted from *Trumpets of Beaten Metal*
by Eugene Laverdiere, p. 6
Liturgical Press, Collegeville, Minn., ©1974

STRESS AND DISTRESS

There are so many things that can cause us stress. Each of us knows what these are in our own lives. For some of us it may be financial strain, or family worries, or health problems, or a combination of many problems. Sometimes it's just a feeling of being out of sorts.

At such times, when emotional distress invades our life, it helps to have someone close to whom we can just talk. Such times are not the occasions when we feel capable of stirring the world with an outburst of oratory. All we want is a friend to talk to — a compassionate, understanding friend who hears us and gives us courage.

Such friends are rare — but there is one such friend available to each and every one of us. God. It doesn't matter if you haven't paid much attention to him in the past. You need him now, and like any true friend, he's always at hand, unobtrusive, but there when you need him.

"Entrust your cares to the Lord, and he will support you" (Psalm 54 [55]:22).

William O'Meara

LIVING COURAGE

Allowing for all differences and normal precautions, there is nothing nobler in old age than true courage: nothing commands greater respect, as long as it is courage and not just senile obstinacy. Age, by convention, is spared many of the rude shocks of youth; but by the same token, if we want to find its true meaning, it must be glorified by the type of courage which is in its own right and suits its own condition.

The question of courage can be summed up in two words: the courage to live, and the courage to love. Said more precisely: the courage to accept our natural life, whatever be its length or circumstances, and the courage to accept the divine life, the life of the resurrection, which is love.

Reflections on Growing Old,
John LaFarge, p. 124

LEAD, KINDLY LIGHT

Lead, kindly Light, amid the encircling
  gloom,
Lead thou me on;
The night is dark, and I am far from
  home,
Lead thou me on;
Keep thou my feet; I do not ask to see
The distant scene; one step enough for me.

I was not ever thus, nor prayed that thou
Shouldst lead me on;
I loved to choose and see my path; but
now
Lead thou me on:
I loved the garish day, and, spite of fears,
Pride ruled my will — remember not past
years.

So long thy power hath blessed me, sure it
still
Will lead me on,
O'er moor and fen, o'er crag and torrent,
till
The night gone,
And with the morn those angel faces
smile,
Which I have loved long since, and lost
awhile.

Cardinal John Henry Newman

Hope

TRANSFIGURED

In his transfiguration Christ showed his disciples the splendor of his beauty, to which he shapes and colors those who are his own.

Saint Thomas Aquinas

IN THE HANDS OF GOD

Whenever we pray with hope, we put our lives in the hands of God. Fear and anxiety fade away and everything we are given and everything we are deprived of is nothing but a finger pointing out the direction of God's hidden promise which we shall taste in full.

With Open Hands
by Henri Nouwen, p. 86
Ave Maria Press, Notre Dame, Ind., ©1972

HOLDING ON IN TRUST

I've had several surgeries myself, never too serious, but I always face the possibilities before going under anesthetic. Sunday week I go in for surgery and I'm more frightened than I've ever been before. It may not be malignant, but we don't know. And I've had skin cancers already. My father died of cancer. All of this is very, very frightening. And, as I say, I faced it to some extent previously, but never fully. The imminent death of all people just seems to close in on me. I think it's just not so much fear as trying to hold to a trust in the power that made us all and who wills our good — and even daring to sense the possibility of further adventure ahead. Life has opened up to me some of the most wonderful adventures really. This leads me to feel that death may be another door. I can't think of it as a stopping of life and of fellowship, but rather as a continuing. I'm trying to hold to this while at the moment I'm inwardly trembling.

Clarice Bowman,
Aging as a Spiritual Journey, p. 249

OPTIMISM AT ITS BEST

One never knows what might have happened to a person trapped by social conditions if religious faith had not channelled his or her anger and frustration. Looking to God, trusting that he has some reason or ultimate design in mind, can lift people out of the squalid and into the ecstatic — if only for a few moments in a beautiful church. Religion is optimism taken to its highest power.

Pathfinders by Gail Sheehy, p. 290
William Morrow & Company, New York, ©1981

GOD GIVES US PEACE

Our Lord told us that he was not giving us his peace as the world gives it. "Do not let your heart be distressed, or play the coward," he said (John 14:27). "The peace of God," Saint Paul tells us, "surpasses all our thinking" (Philippians 4:7). It is woven of trust and cushioned with silence. It bears no relation to the ready-made consolations and the delusive hopes that are served out so freely to the old and the sick. They are children, if you like, but it is the Lord himself who is going to rock them to sleep.

The peace of God talks less and means more. It should be treated with gentleness and with respect.

The Lord Is Near,
Paul-Marie Richaud, pp. 29-30

HOPING

Hope means to keep living
amid desperation
and to keep humming
in the darkness.
Hoping is knowing that there is love,
it is trust in tomorrow
it is falling asleep
and waking again
when the sun rises.

In the midst of a gale at sea,
it is to discover land.
In the eyes of another
it is to see that he understands you.
... As long as there is still hope
there will also be prayer.
... And God will be holding you
in his hands.

With Open Hands,
Henri Nouwen, p. 85

Love

FAITH AND LOVE ARE ONE

Faith is the beginning and the end is love, and God is the two of them brought into unity.

Saint Ignatius of Antioch

SOUL TO SOUL

A smile is the shortest path from one soul to another.

Translated from
Brother Bernard Marie, OFS
L'Ange de Tobie, p. 233

LOVE HURTS

Now I find that sharing is not all joy... Is that what it means to love someone else as yourself? That their hurts, hurt you? As if your heart were broken?

An Everyday God, by James Taylor, p. 105
Wood Lake Books and The Upper Room
Winfield, B.C., and Nashville, Tenn. ©1981

POWER OF LOVE

Since these are rather apocalyptic days — people phone me and ask if the end of the world is not coming — it is well for us all, young and old, to remember that the matter upon which we shall be questioned

at the Last Judgment is precisely the degree to which we have, or have not, tangibly shown the love of neighbor. "Did you visit me when I was destitute, when I was sick, when I was in prison...?"

Reflections on Growing Old,
John LaFarge, p. 52

LOVING ONE'S NEIGHBORS

I think one of the reasons we tend to reach out more to the anonymous than the known is that it is safer. We don't have to get as emotionally involved. The pain of rejection is not as great. We're not risking as much. To get deeply involved with someone we know can be a hazardous undertaking. Ministering to John or Jane Doe could be relatively easy, but ministering to my best friend or my son can be extremely difficult.

Let our ministry and charity begin at home. I am not saying it should end there. And I am including in the "home" territory all those we already know — not only our families, but our friends, our co-workers, our neighbors on the block.

Some of these may be in great need. There may be deep hurts we can help heal. Let's not limit our charity to the anonymous of the world.

Joy Comes with the Morning,
William Kinnaird, p. 86

NEW OPPORTUNITY TO LOVE

Age strips you of certain joys and privileges. But of the greatest privilege, age, as a rule, cannot wholly rob you. Advanced years give an extra opportunity to make the love of your neighbor your own, in new and unexpected ways, and one way is the relief of loneliness for other aged persons. Modern means of communication have, indeed, done much to decrease the terrors of loneliness, but they have not entirely abolished it. Few are the aged who do not suffer from solitude in some degree. The longer you live, the more of your old friends and acquaintances drop off. The more frequently do you pick up the paper and read the death notices of folk considerably younger than yourself. Or you just drift apart.

Yet you can do much to mitigate the bitter loneliness of old age; you can at least ease its frightening, absolute character. Such simple means of communication are available as a casual note or letter, a short visit, remembrance of an anniversary; or, from time to time, a longer conversation, where again you can check over the past. Or the telephone call.

How much can be accomplished by an occasional visit, an opportunity to talk of old acquaintances, a bit of the hundred-and-one ways by which a spark of sunshine may be brought into desolate lives! So much comfort comes from feeling yourself as somehow a member of a group, however small and apparently unimportant: so much can be obtained for so little.

Adapted from *Reflections on Growing Old,*
John LaFarge, pp. 53, 54, 55

TEACH US TO TOUCH

Teach us to reach out and touch, Lord!
To hold each other in love
and to cuddle in affection;
to embrace in friendship
and to hug with laughter;
to support each other in grief
and to rejoice in celebration;
to walk hand-in-hand by the sea
and to sit snuggled up by the fire.
Teach us to touch.

Through the Darkness; The Psalms of a Survivor
by Christine Frye, p. 62
Wood Lake Books, Winfield, B.C. [1983]

TAKEN BEYOND OURSELVES

There is, hidden or flaunted, a sword between the sexes till an entire marriage reconciles them...

And then one or other dies. And we think of this as love cut short; like a dance stopped in mid-career or a flower with its head unluckily snapped off — something truncated and therefore lacking its due shape. I wonder. If, as I can't help suspecting, the dead also feel the pains of separation (and this may be one of their purgatorial sufferings), then for both lovers, and for all pairs of lovers without exception, bereavement is a universal and integral part of our experience of love. It follows marriage as normally as marriage follows courtship or as autumn follows summer. It is not a truncation of the process but one of its phases; not the interruption of the dance but the next figure. We are "taken out of ourselves" by the loved one while she is here. Then comes the tragic figure of the dance in which we must learn to be still taken out of ourselves though the bodily presence is withdrawn, to love the very Her, and not fall back to loving our past, or our memory, or our sorrow, or our relief from sorrow, or our own love.

A Grief Observed
by C. S. Lewis, pp. 40-41
Faber and Faber, London, 1964
[Published in U.S.A. by Seabury, 1963]

LEARNING TO BE ALONE

Loneliness is not simply a matter of being alone; loneliness is the feeling that nobody else truly cares what happens to us. The loneliness of the elderly has become a source of unhappiness to society — yet life should have taught older people how to deal with loneliness, how to prepare, how to cope, and how to use it effectively. What we do not do for ourselves, no one can do for us. We must be responsible even for our own loneliness. For our own sake, we must learn to be alone.

Adapted from
Trust in God... But Tie Your Camel,
Sylvia McDonald, pp. 96-97

TO SEE AS GOD SEES

It is often thought that the dead see us. And we assume, whether reasonably or not, that if they see us at all they see us more clearly than before. Does H. [the author's deceased wife] now see exactly how much froth and tinsel there was in what she called, and I call, my love? So be it. Look your hardest, dear. I wouldn't hide it if I could. We didn't idealize each other. We tried to keep no secrets. You knew most of the rotten places in me already. If you now see anything worse, I can take it. So can you. Rebuke, explain, mock, forgive. For this is one of the miracles of love; it gives — to both, but perhaps especially to the woman — a power of seeing through its own enchantments and yet not being disenchanted.

To see, in some measure, like God. His love and his knowledge are not distinct from one another, nor from him. We could almost say he sees because he loves, and therefore loves although he sees.

A Grief Observed,
C. S. Lewis, pp. 56-57

RESURGAM

I shall say, Lord, "Is it music, is it
  morning,
Song that is fresh as sunrise, light that
  sings?"
When on some hill there breaks the
  immortal warning
Of half-forgotten springs.

I shall say, Lord, "I have loved you, not
  another,
Heard in all quiet your footsteps on my
  road,
Felt your strong shoulder near me, O my
  brother,
Lightening the load."

I shall say, Lord, "I remembered, working,
sleeping,
One face I looked for, one denied and
dear.
Now that you come my eyes are blind with
weeping,
But you will kiss them clear."

I shall say, Lord, "Touch my lips, and so
unseal them;
I have learned silence since I lived and
died."
I shall say, Lord, "Lift my hands, and so
reveal them,
Full, satisfied."

I shall say, Lord, "We will laugh again
tomorrow,
Now we'll be still a little, friend with friend.
Death was the gate and the long way was
sorrow.
Love is the end."

Marjorie L. C. Pickthall

Death

DISCOVERING THE WAY

When we have travelled all ways, we shall come to the end of all ways, who says, "I am the Way."

Saint Ambrose

ASLEEP IN THE LORD

What is death at most? It is a journey for a season; a sleep longer than usual. If you fear death, you should then also fear sleep.

Saint John Chrysostom

JUST MOVED

An old doctor lived in the community who was not licensed, he was not school trained. He made his own medicine, carried in his bag, but he got people well. They loved him. He could cure their headaches, and he could cool their temperatures. That old man got people well, with no degree, giving the glory to God.

Some people went up in wagons on Saturday to see the old doctor, and he was not home, and they stood there amazed, bothered and disturbed, wondering where the old doctor had gone. An old man came by and they asked him if he knew where the doctor had gone and he said, "Read the sign. He left a sign on his door — read it." And they began to read the sign.

They are going to read your sign and they are going to read mine one day. And you know what the sign said? The old doctor left it there: "Still in business, just moved upstairs."

"An Affirmation of Life"
by Martin Luther King, Senior
Spiritual Well-Being of the Elderly, p. 86

DEATH'S GENTLE REMINDER

All that you are and all that you've done and been is culminated in your death. When you're dying, if you're fortunate enough to have some prior warning (other than that we all have all the time if we come to terms with our finiteness), you get your final chance to grow, to become more truly who you really are, to become more fully human. But you don't need to nor should you wait until death is at your doorstep before you really start to live. If you can begin to see death as an invisible, but friendly, companion on your life's journey — gently reminding you not to wait till tomorrow to do what you mean to do —

then you can learn to live your life rather than simply passing through it.

Death: The Final Stage of Growth
by Elisabeth Kübler-Ross, p. x
Prentice-Hall, Englewood Cliffs, N.J., ©1975

PASSING THROUGH

In the last century an American tourist visited the renowned Polish Rabbi Hofetz Chaim. The tourist was amazed to find the rabbi's home only a simple room, filled with books, a table and a bench.

"Rabbi," he asked, "where is your furniture?"

"Where is yours?" asked the rabbi.

"Mine?" asked the puzzled American. "But I'm only a visitor here. I'm only passing through."

"So am I," replied the rabbi.

"Walking Without Fainting"
by Thomas C. Cook, Senior,
Spiritual Well-Being of the Elderly, p. 74

LET'S GET GOING

Sometimes I will begin — not often — a meditation on my own death, not as a fearful thing, but as a reminder. The net result of it is to really relish what is here right now. It is not something that I look forward

to. Maybe some people reach that stage toward wholeness and wisdom where they are yearning for that great moment. When I think about death and reflect on it, it acts as a means of reminding me, "Let's get going here."

Daniel O'Hanlon,
Aging as a Spiritual Journey, p. 248

BLOSSOMING

I used to think a lot about life after death and about reuniting with one's family and all of that. It might be a totally different world. It might be this world transformed. I do not think that I can imagine it. I believe in it. It is going to be a blossoming out, an opening out into this something new and glorious.

Anita Caspary,
Aging as a Spiritual Journey, p. 258

NEITHER ENEMY NOR PRISON

Death is not an enemy to be conquered or a prison to be escaped. It is an integral part of our lives that gives meaning to human existence. It sets a limit on our time in this life, urging us on to do something productive with that time as long as it is ours to use.

Death: The Final Stage of Growth,
Elisabeth Kübler-Ross, p. x

MOST FAVORABLE MOMENT

We must believe steadfastly in the divine wisdom. The Lord only takes his children at the moment which, his mercy tempering his justice, he thinks most favorable for coming to seek them. He sometimes appears like a flash of lightning, it is true. He warned us of it. Sometimes a sick man, even on his deathbed, is taken just when it seemed least likely. But the divine effulgence lights up the soul. That soul can, if it is on the wrong path, turn around in an instant toward the Lord. We have no right to despair of the eternal fate of any of our dead.

The Lord Is Near,
Paul-Marie Richaud, pp. 41-43

CONSECRATED IN DEATH

Death is no mere escape, even for those who have been awaiting it impatiently. It is the synthesis of all the activities that have preceded it; it is the sacrifice of all sacrifices, and finally it is the absolute, complete and crowning act of love. It is a consecration.

The Lord Is Near,
Paul-Marie Richaud, p. 43

LIFE GIVES THANKS FOR LIFE

It is no mere chance that the chrism itself, by which the sick are anointed, is blessed by the bishop at the high altar of the cathedral on the solemn day, Holy Thursday, when the Church commemorates the opening scene in the final act of the great drama of the redemption and resurrection.

In the phenomenon of death, we are drawn into fellowship with all humanity, with all creation. We are steadfastly drawn into companionship with the development of the entire cosmos. In her sacramental ministrations, the Church draws us more closely than ever into her fellowship. All that the Church has is ours, as never before. The gift of the Viaticum, the sacramental Body and Blood of the Savior, in that last hour is a gift of perfect thanksgiving: the Lord giving thanks within us for the infinitely precious gift of life itself.

When we leave, our final and most solemn act is simply and humbly to thank him for that gift, which itself is the meaning of old age, and to regret that we have not used it better.

Why, then, should we hesitate to talk of these things? Isn't it better to discuss them frequently, to clarify our thoughts, to rid ourselves of false fears, to settle upon those points that are essential? And we all profit by one another's experience.

Reflections on Growing Old,
John LaFarge, pp. 136-37

GOD TAKES US

Why talk about death, it may be asked, to people to whom the subject may be a torture? I should like the pages that do talk about death to be the most comforting in the whole of this little book.

We do not go of our own. It is God who takes us.

The Lord takes us to him, into his glory, into his own happiness. If he takes back the earthly life he had given us, it is only to admit us wholly into that eternal life which is his own. When Saint Charles Borromeo was archbishop of Milan, he did not want death to be portrayed in his palace with a scythe but with a golden key. Sister Elizabeth of the Trinity said: "As I see it, death is this wall collapsing and I falling into the arms of my Beloved."

Death is a resurrection, a new birth, a new baptism... "Do you hear the bell?" cried the long-deaf Beethoven on his deathbed. The life of grace, which we received with the baptismal water, the supernatural life, is going at last to burst into full and final bloom, as full as our last living act is filled with the love of God. Jean du Plessis, the hero of the First World War battle of Dixmude, was right when he couched his prayer in these words: "O God, let me all the days of my life look on my grave as my cradle, for there I shall be born a second time, and there death will lay me down and leave me for ever."

The Lord Is Near,
Paul-Marie Richaud, pp. 41-42

CROSSING THE BAR

Sunset and evening star,
And one clear call for me!
And may there be no moaning of the bar,
When I put out to sea,

But such a tide as moving seems asleep,
Too full for sound and foam,
When that which drew from out the boundless deep
Turns again home.

Twilight and evening bell,
And after that the dark!
And may there be no sadness of farewell,
When I embark;

For tho' from out our bourne of Time and
 Place
 The flood may bear me far,
I hope to see my Pilot face to face
 When I have crost the bar.

Alfred Lord Tennyson

Indexes

Scripture Texts and References

Old Testament

New Testament

Authors

Titles of Books, Hymns and Poems

Prayers

Themes

Acknowledgments

Companion on Life's Journey was inspired by the spirit and contents of **L'Ange de Tobie; messe, prières, et pensées pour nos vieux jours,** with texts selected, translated and edited by Brother Bernard-Marie, Third Order of St. Francis. **L'Ange de Tobie,** copyright ©1985 by Editions du Chalet, Paris, is distributed in North America by Novalis, Ottawa (Canada).

Permission to reprint the following passages in **Companion on Life's Journey** is gratefully acknowledged:

pp. 13-50 from **Living with Christ,** introductions to Sundays and feasts, Sept. 4, 1977 - Oct. 6, 1985. Published nine times a year by Novalis, Ottawa. Copyright by Novalis, St. Paul University, Ottawa.

pp. 63, 79-80, 100, from **Time Out; Prayers for Busy People,** by Basil Arbour. Published by Novalis, Ottawa. Copyright by Novalis, St. Paul University, Ottawa.

pp. 213-14, 251-2, 265-6, from **Aging as a Spiritual Journey** by Eugene C. Bianchi. Published by the Crossroad Publishing Company, New York. Copyright ©1982 by Eugene C. Bianchi. Reprinted by permission of The Crossroad Publishing Company.

pp. 214, 260, from **Trust in God... But Tie Your Camel** by Sister Sylvia McDonald, CND. Published by Novalis, Ottawa. Copyright ©1983 by Novalis, St. Paul University, Ottawa.

pp. 215, 217, 223-24, 232-36, from **The Bible Speaks on Aging** by Frank Stagg. Published by Broadman Press, Nashville, Tennessee. Copyright ©1981 by Broadman Press. All rights reserved. Used by permission, courtesy The Sunday School Board of the Southern Baptist Convention.

pp. 215-16, 238-39, from **Growing Old, and How to Cope with It** by Alfons Deeken. Published by Paulist Press, New York. Copyright ©1972 by The Missionary Society of St. Paul the Apostle in the State of New York. Reprinted courtesy of the publisher.

pp. 218, 221-22, 232-33, 263-65, from **Spiritual Well-Being of the Elderly.** National Intra-Decade Conference on Spiritual Well-Being of the Elderly, Atlanta, Georgia, 1977. Edited by James A. Thorson and Thomas C. Cook, Jr. Copyright ©1980, Charles C. Thomas, Publisher, Springfield, Illinois. Reprinted courtesy of the publisher.

pp. 219-20, 256, from **Joy Comes with the Morning; A Handbook of Christian Encouragement and Affirmation** by William M. Kinnaird. Published by Word Books, Waco, Texas, 1980. Copyright ©1979 by the author. Reprinted courtesy of the author.

pp. 224-25, 237-38, 243-44, 246, from **Towards Evening** by Mary Hope. Sheed and Ward, London, 1956. All rights reserved. Reprinted by permission of the publisher.

pp. 225-27, 230-31, 240-41, 244-45, 253, 267, 269-70, from **The Lord Is Near** by Cardinal Paul-Marie Richaud. Translated by Ronald Matthews. Published 1958 by Geoffrey Chapman, London, a division of Cassell Ltd. All rights reserved. Reprinted by permission.

pp. 227-30, 245-46, 249, 255-58, 268-69, from **Reflections on Growing Old** by Father John LaFarge, SJ. Published by Doubleday, Garden City, New York. Copyright ©1963 by The America Press. Reprinted by permission of Doubleday & Company, Inc.

p. 247, from **Trumpets of Beaten Metal** by Eugene Laverdiere. Published by The Liturgical Press, Collegeville, Minnesota. Copyright ©1974 by The Order of St. Benedict, Inc. Used with permission.

pp. 251, 253-54, from **With Open Hands** by Henri J. M. Nouwen. Published by Ave Maria Press, Notre Dame, Indiana. Copyright ©1972 by Ave Maria Press. Reprinted courtesy of the publisher.

p. 252, from **Pathfinders** by Gail Sheehy. Published by William Morrow and Company, New York. Copyright ©1981 by Gail Sheehy. Reprinted courtesy or the publisher.

p. 255, from **An Everyday God,** by James Taylor. Published by Wood Lake Books, Inc., Winfield, British Columbia, and The Upper Room, Nashville, Tennessee. Copyright ©1981 by the author. Reprinted courtesy of the publishers.

p. 258, from **Through the Darkness; The Psalms of a Survivor** by Christine Frye. Published by Wood Lake Books, Inc., Winfield, British Columbia. Copyright by the author. Reprinted courtesy of the publisher.

pp. 258-61, from **A Grief Observed** by C. S. Lewis. Published by Faber & Faber, London, 1964; Seabury, Greenwich, Connecticut, 1963. Copyright ©1961 by C. S. Lewis. Reprinted by permission of Faber & Faber, Ltd., London, and Harper & Row, New York.

pp. 264-66, from **Death: The Final Stage of Growth** by Elisabeth Kübler-Ross. Published by Prentice-Hall, Englewood Cliffs, New Jersey. Copyright ©1975 by Elisabeth Kübler-Ross. Reprinted by permission of the publisher.

The editor and publishers also thank Roslyn Brown, director of pastoral care, St. Patrick's Home, Ottawa; Dr. Frank J. Henderson, Edmonton, Alberta, past chairperson of the National Council for Liturgy (Canada); Sister Sylvia McDonald, CND, co-ordinator, Marianopolis Retirement Centre, Montreal; and William O'Meara, senior English-language editor at Novalis, Ottawa, for their advice and assistance.